Endpapers: Viking chessmen found on the Isle of Lewis in the Outer Hebrides, from a set in the British Museum

PURNELL LIBRARY OF KNOWLEDGE

The Vikings

SBN 361 02106 2
Published 1973 by Purnell
© 1973 Purnell & Sons Ltd.
Made and printed in Italy

The Vikings

By Kenneth Allen

Foreword by Paul Johnstone
Member of the Council for Nautical Archaeology

PURNELL
London

FOREWORD

In Greenland, on a short stretch of grass by a clear stream full of fish, stand the thick turf foundations of one of the most romantic ruins in the world. It is the farmhouse of Eirik the Red, the Norseman who led the colonization of Greenland in 986 A.D. A few miles away is the church of Hvalsey, the most westerly of all Gothic buildings, nearer to the United States than Europe. From here other hardy Norse sailors went on to "Vinland", on the mainland of America. So for three centuries the Vikings ranged from that continent across the North Atlantic to Scandinavia, down the great rivers of Russia to Byzantium, and from the icy North cape to the shores of Sicily, rivalled only by the Polynesians as the greatest sailors in history. Often they came with their bearded axes as "priest-murderers", so that to this day Ireland is studded with the tall stone towers the monks built for the look-outs to ring the warning bells that the fury of the northmen was coming. Storms then were a welcome gift from God, because no longships would dare venture out on the rough seas. So powerful was the impact of these terrifying vessels that when the monks carved Noah's Arks on their High Crosses, they made them in the shape of Viking longships with the dove perched on the mast amidships!

But the same men who set sail from the Scandinavian countries to pillage and plunder in many parts of Europe were at other times peaceful settlers and traders; and we know from the lucky chance of the blue clay which has preserved some of their ship burials that there were among the Vikings great artists who carved their strange twining animals with extraordinary skill. Warriors, colonisers, traders in goods from white falcons to hazelnuts, wood carvers, navigators—these are the people the author portrays, the people who form such an important part of our own ancestry.

Paul Johnstone

CONTENTS

WHO WERE THE VIKINGS?

Viking invaders: the sight that was to strike terror on many European shores for almost three hundred years

UNLIKE MANY other periods in history, the Viking Age is clearly defined. It began with the first attack of the Northmen in 793 AD upon the religious centre of Lindisfarne in north-east England and ended in the year with the familiar date—1066.

The name "Viking" was given to the men of Norway, Sweden and Denmark that today we know as Scandinavia. How the Vikings got their name, however, is not so clear. Today most historians agree that it is derived from "vik", meaning a bay or inlet, the place where these early sea-rovers set out on expeditions that were to take them to Britain, France, Spain and the Mediterranean, to Russia, Iceland, Greenland and even America.

To go "a-viking", meant to leave home and sail off in search of adventure. It was used in a sense, as today people talk of going "camping" but, as it is incorrect to give them all the name of "campers", when otherwise they are engaged in a wide variety of professions, so it is wrong to call every Scandinavian in those days a "Viking". He was only a Viking when he was

Viking plunder? A complete armlet (left), fragments of others, and a single strap end (centre left), all of silver, from the treasure hoard of a Viking army found in the North of England. The armlets had been deliberately broken up, ready for the melting pot

actually raiding, or sailing to or from the objects of his plunder. At home, he returned to being a farmer, trader or craftsman. In any case, going a-viking was perfectly respectable. Fighting was part of everyday life and stealing was commonplace, provided one stole from an enemy and not a friend.

The Viking leader gathered his crews from free men, each bringing his own food or paying a share towards the common fund. There were no wages. Instead, each man agreed in advance to a share of the results of the voyage, and sealed it by a handshake. Hence the men accepted in this fashion were called "hands".

At the beginning of the 9th century Charles the Great (Charlemagne) was ruling a vast empire that consisted of Italy, Gaul and much of Spain and Germany which he protected with fortresses and garrisons. In consequence, there were few attacks by sea-rovers during his reign. Other countries were not so strong. England and Ireland were divided into a number of small kingdoms, all ruled by petty kings, and Scotland consisted of constantly warring clans.

The Scandinavian people had been trading very profitably with the countries bordering the Baltic Sea, yet their young men had a restless urge to explore further afield.

The coasts of Britain bordered rich arable lands that lay warm, open and defenceless—so different from their cold, inhospitable, and overcrowded country with its poor soil. It was inevitable that before long Viking longships should run up on to a quiet and accessible beach of north-east England.

On the day that happened the Viking Age can be said to have begun.

The Viking Raids Begin

The year 793 brought dreadful omens and portents. Evil signs were to be seen in the troubled sky over Northumbria, a terrible storm threw balls of fire through the air and the night sky was torn with jagged lightning. When a stream of blood poured from the roof of St. Peter's in York a priest quoted Jeremiah saying, "Out of the North an evil shall break forth upon all inhabitants of the land".

The "evil" broke on a summer's day in June, 793. A number of young men from Norway, looking for water and fresh meat, ran their boats on to the shingle of the Holy Isle of Lindisfarne, a place famous for its monastery which housed the bones of St. Cuthbert, the great Northern Saint. Whooping and shouting, they ran ashore. When the monks tried to stop them taking their livestock, they were cut down. The monastery was sacked of its gold and silver plate and its rich hangings, and then, leaving burning buildings and dead bodies behind them, the striped sails of the raiders' ships disappeared over the horizon. The brief raid, with its murder and looting, was similar in many ways to those of the Tudor sea-dogs, five and a half centuries later. The earlier raids, however, did not mean that Christian killed Christian, but that Norsemen, with their own fierce religion of gods and goddesses, killed men who in their eyes were "heathens".

The young men returned home, proudly showed the valuable loot and remarked that the monks from whom it was taken did not defend themselves, but stood to be butchered like cattle.

The following year another attack was launched, again on Northumbria, but this time against Jarrow, on the mainland. This was beaten off, however, and for some years the Vikings did not return to Britain but concentrated on Ireland and the islands off Scotland.

In 834 they returned in force to attack, not helpless communities, but strong towns, including London and York. The great booty that was gained encouraged others to follow. Large fleets were fitted out and hardly a year passed without an attack taking place somewhere in England.

The year 865, however, saw something new. This time the Vikings arrived, not to plunder but to settle, and this time the invading army consisted of more Danes than Norsemen. They arrived on the East Anglian coast, fortified their camp and went into quarters for the winter. Spring brought more ships from Denmark and the army marched inland. After several years of war East Anglia was conquered, becoming a Danish kingdom. Another force moved into Wessex where battle after battle was fought with the stubborn Saxons. The most famous of these was at Ashdown where the King, Aethelred, prayed for victory whilst his brother Alfred led the fighting. At Eastertide, 871, Aethelred died and Alfred became king.

But by then the Danes were virtually masters of the land. One of their leaders, Halfdan, ruled from London, minting coins that bore his likeness. Two years later he was to move north to begin the first system of Viking colonization in England.

Warrior figures brandishing axes, carved on a cross-slab at Lindisfarne Monastery, commemorate the Viking attack

ALFRED AND THE DANELAW

ALFRED WAS called King of Wessex but his title meant little. The Danes were already masters of Northumbria, East Anglia, and Mercia and had also spilled into his kingdom to hold several of his towns. He was forced to buy peace from them, hoping to gain time to bring his army up to strength, yet, despite this, a large fleet of Danish ships appeared near the mouth of the River Exe. When off Swanage, however, a sudden storm sank more than 120 of the ships and the rest sailed away.

A large Danish army later encamped at Dorchester, however, and from this headquarters began to make a series of raids upon the surrounding countryside. At the same time, Halfdan divided a large area of Mercia into five parts, each with a fortified town, or "borough", as its capital. These were to become the Five Boroughs of Stamford, Leicester, Derby, Nottingham and Lincoln. Together with the other Danish settlements in East Anglia, Northumbria, and the south-east Midlands, the total area occupied by the Danes ran from the Humber to the Wash, roughly bordered in the West by the old Roman road called Watling Street. This territory was to become known as the Danelaw, having entirely Danish laws, language, religion and customs.

Halfdan was now determined to bring the kingdom of Alfred under

King Alfred supervises the building of Britain's first navy

Danish rule also. He already had a large army, and in 878 a fleet of 23 ships arrived from Denmark crowded with reinforcements. Greatly outnumbered, Alfred was forced to go into hiding on Athelney, an island protected by swamps and marshes which were quick to drown all who did not know the secret ways across them. Alfred slowly built up his forces and when at last he faced the Danes in battle shortly after Easter he succeeded in routing them completely at Ethandune, in Essex. Many of the defeated Danes agreed to be baptised and were later allowed to settle peacefully in East Anglia.

This victory allowed Alfred fourteen years in which to strengthen his defences and build up a large army. Even more important, he did something that no English king had ever done before. He decided to build a navy of his own in order to rob the Viking ships of their advantage. As the chronicler records: "King Alfred had longships built to go out against the Vikings. They were almost twice as long as the Norsemen's boats. Some had sixty oarsmen, some even more. His ships were faster than those of the Vikings, were more seaworthy and higher".

Few men of Wessex had enough experience to man these ships, however, so Alfred was forced to hire Frisians, natives of what is known today as Holland, while his own seamen gradually learned their trade in the new ships.

Inevitably the Vikings returned. In 892 they swarmed ashore from 250 ships, bringing this time their own

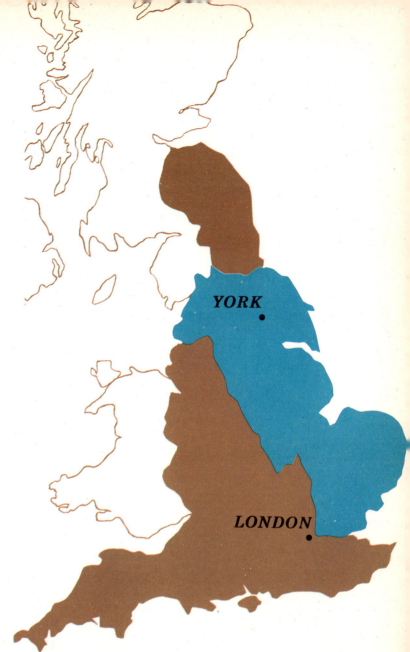

England divided: the Danelaw (coloured blue on the map) with its capital at York, included Northumbria, East Anglia, and the Five Boroughs of Stamford, Leicester, Derby, Nottingham, and Lincoln; Alfred, whose territories lay to the north and south, kept London

horses which formerly they had hoped to capture after landing.

A great many battles were fought, both on land and at sea. Finally, a treaty was signed in which the country became half Saxon, ruled by Alfred, and half Danish, ruled by the Danish leader, Guthrum. Most of the Danes settled peaceably in the Danelaw; but some sailed away to look for a country which did not have such a strong king as Alfred the "Great".

THE VIKINGS IN IRELAND

"THE OCEAN poured torrents of foreigners over Erin, so that not a harbour or landing, fort or stronghold, was without fleets of Scandinavians and pirates". So wrote a monk in 820 in the *Annals of Ulster*.

The first Vikings arrived in Ireland in 795 and the tales they took back to Norway of wealthy, but poorly defended, monasteries and churches, brought shiploads of their fellows. The religious centres of Ireland held the country's most valuable treasures, including jewellery and ornaments in magnificent silver-gilt metalwork. The Great Church at Armagh, for example, was repeatedly plundered. More than wealth lured the invaders, however. The rich soil and the mild climate of the country were a great invitation to settle and in 839, Turgeis, first of the Norwegian sea-kings, arrived to make his home in Dublin and became "king of all the strangers in Erin".

Curiously, he called himself Abbot of Armagh, although he tried to replace Christianity with the worship of Thor. His wife, Ota even carried out heathen ceremonies at the cathedral's high altar. But the Norsemen realized that the Irish people were as proud and independent as themselves and certainly did not wish to live in peace with the invaders. Turgeis only ruled for six years; then the Irish rose against him, captured him and threw him into Lough Owel where he drowned.

Turgeis's remaining followers were hounded down and gradually weakened in a series of battles, and for a time the Irish seemed to have regained their independence. But a new threat appeared: more Vikings landed, this time from Denmark. The Danish Vikings had no allegiance to their Norwegian counterparts, however, and lost no time in seizing Dublin from them. The Norwegians retaliated by trying to destroy the Danish fleet, and the Irish seem to have found a Viking 'civil war' on their front doorstep.

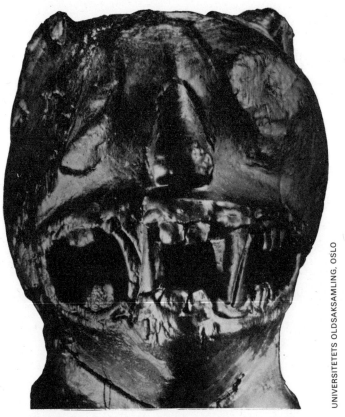

Horrific symbol of the Norse invasion: a demon head, carved in wood, from a long-buried Viking ship

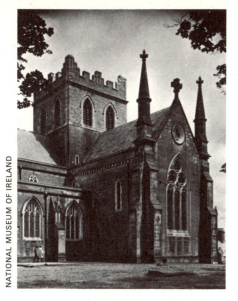

Above: St. Patrick's Church, Armagh, today, on the site of the Great Church so often pillaged by the Vikings; right: a Viking longboat. The network of ropes which strengthened the sail made it appear chequered

But not long afterwards, a new fleet of Norwegians arrived under the command of Olaf, the king of Norway's son. Olaf managed to command the loyalty of both Norwegians and Danes, and, as Viking leader, settled peaceably there for a number of years, ruling from Dublin.

During this time the Vikings also established trading centres on the inlets of the south and west coasts, where they could make full use of their ships, at Limerick, Wexford, Cork and Waterford. There are few traces of colonization elsewhere in Ireland.

In 901 the Irish drove the Vikings from their homes and it was twelve years before they returned to rule, this time for another seventy years. The last king, Olaf Kvaran from Northumbria, ruled in York as well as Dublin. He was defeated at a great battle at Tara in 980 and, whilst his capital burned furiously behind him, he fled to the monastery on Iona and became a monk.

In 1002 Ireland became united for the first time under an Irish King, the great Brian Boru. After twelve years of a peaceful reign, Irish and Vikings met for the last time in battle. Men came from other Norse colonies—even from Flanders and Normandy—to fight under the magic raven banner of Sigurd Digri. The battle was fought at Clontarf and although Brian Boru and Sigurd were both killed, the Irish gained the victory.

An exciting saga of the battle, written by a warrior who was present, contains the lines:

I was there when warriors fought
Sword blades rang on Ireland's coast
Metal yelled as shield it sought
Spear points in the well-armed host . . .

And that was the end of the Viking rule in Ireland.

INTO EUROPE AND BEYOND

THE SPIRIT of adventure which had taken the Vikings to Britain encouraged others to sail southwards to the rich countries of Western Europe. Whilst it was principally the Norsemen who were to settle in the Atlantic islands and in Ireland, it was to be the Danes who settled in the east of England and the northern coast of France.

The first Viking raids on the Carolingian empire of Charlemagne were unsuccessful and when he died in 814 his son, Louis the Pious, continued to maintain the strong defences, with ships patrolling off the coast and with shore garrisons ready to deal with any invaders. But in time Louis was faced with troubles within his kingdom, including having to fight his own son, Lothar. In consequence the country was weakened and its defences slowly crumbled as men were taken away to fight elsewhere.

In 834 the Vikings, who had been watching and waiting, struck at the coast of Friesland, today known as Holland. The capital city was Dorestad, situated south-west of Utrecht, near a tributary of the Rhine. It was considered the largest and wealthiest trading centre in Northern Europe. They met with no resistance and, when the news of their success reached Denmark, great fleets of ships sailed at once, turning their carved prows towards this and other wealthy European sea and river ports.

One fleet was led by a great hero, Ragnar Lodbrok. With 120 longships he sailed up the Seine to attack and plunder Paris. Another fleet of 600 ships moved up the Elbe to plunder Hamburg. Lothar, the new ruler of the Empire, hoping to fight fire with fire, gave the island of Walcharen in Friesland to two brothers, Harald and Rorik, on condition that they kept other Vikings away.

The procession of Viking longships continued. Bordeaux, Toulouse, Tours, Rouen and many other French cities were plundered and, says the chronicler with a sense of utter despair, "Scarcely a town, or monastery is spared. All the people fly and there are few who dare to say 'Stay and fight, for our land, children and homes'. In their trance, preoccupied with rivalry, they ransom for tribute what they sought to defend with the sword, and allow the kingdom of the Christian to perish".

There was hardly a river in Western Europe—Seine, Loire, Garonne, Maas, Scheldt and the Rhine—where the waters were not churned to foam by the oars of the dreaded longships.

No army, it seemed, was strong enough to stem the flood of plundering Vikings. Finally Charles the Bald, king of France, decided to bribe them to

Ragnar Lodbrok and his fleet of longships attack 9th century Paris. Although Ragnar took much booty and many prisoners, he failed, like all the other Viking fleets after him, to capture the city

go and leave his country in peace. For the first time a king offered "Danegeld" a system of payment that was later to be used in England. Yet still the raids went on and it was at this time that the pitiful prayer of Christians everywhere was heard—*A furore Normannorum libera nos*—"From the fury of the Northmen, Oh Lord, deliver us".

The Swedes Strike East

When the Vikings spoke of their great voyages they said that they had gone *Vestrveg*, to the West, or *Austrveg*, to

the East. To a large extent, the Norwegians and Danes took the first route, going "a-viking" to Britain and the surrounding islands, the empire of Charlemagne, to Spain and the Mediterranean. The Swedes took the other which led them to the Baltic regions, to Russia, Constantinople and the Near East.

The Swedes were great traders but, instead of taking the sea route like the others, took their boats along the ice-fringed rivers of the Volga, Dnieper and others. They travelled through great expanses of bleak, open country, on

A Persian trading post of the 9th and 10th centuries. The Danish merchant is bargaining with some Turks over his furs and female slaves. The slave trade was not confined to the East: Hedeby, in Denmark, was an internationally-known slave market

fast flowing water between high, snow-capped mountains, or past huge primeval forests. This was the land of the fierce tribes of Finns and Slavs whose main wealth was furs and slaves, honey and wax.

The Swedes came at last to the Black Sea and to the Caspian Sea where they unloaded their goods for immediate sale or for the caravans to take them on to the great trading centres of the Eastern World.

The chronicles record how the first of these adventurers arrived in 830 and were brought before the Emperor Theophilus in Byzantium. It must have been

a strange meeting when these tough, bearded warriors from Northern Europe came face to face with an Oriental monarch and his elegant, scented court.

Some years later a writer declared "I have never seen humans more nobly built. They are as tall as palm trees, red blonde, with light skins. They wear neither shirt nor coat with sleeves. The man wears a cape slung over one shoulder, so that one hand is free. Every man carries an axe, a dirk, and a sword. You never see them without these weapons. . . ."

So great an impression did they make

that many were recruited as officers of the Imperial Guard; the others who preferred to continue a life of greater freedom became known as the chiefs of the caravans of traders, coming each year to Constantinople by the "Great Waterway".

By building up important trade routes to the East the Swedish traders brought great wealth back to their Northern homes, including brocades, jewellery, spices and wine. Some of this jewellery has been found in their graves together with—and this was an exciting find—a coin of the Emperor Theophilus (829–842).

One of the tribes of the Swedish nation settled in and around the great trading centres of Kiev and Novgorod. They were known as "men of Rus" which, it is believed, comes from the Finnish word for Sweden—*Ruotsi*. This in turn is from *rodsmen* meaning "rowers" or "men of the oar-way". In time, these "men of Rus" were to give their name to the vast wilderness of a country which they had opened up to the outside world . . . Russia.

Longships in the Mediterranean

During the middle of the 9th century Vikings pushed down the coast of Europe until they came to the rich countries of Spain and Portugal then ruled by the Moors. The first recorded raid took place in 844 when Vikings from Ireland and the Hebrides followed the coast until, reaching the town of La Coruña, they jumped ashore and stormed into battle. But they were out-numbered and outfought and were forced back to their ships. Soon their scarlet sails which, as a writer of the time said, gave the appearance of "the sea being covered with dark red birds", slipped away into the twilight. Angered at this repulse, the Vikings reached Lisbon, stormed and captured it, then moved on to plunder Cadiz and later Seville. By then, however, they had lost a large part of their men and ships, and were forced to return to Ireland.

A few years later a more ambitious expedition left Brittany. Sixty-two long-ships were commanded by two experienced Vikings, Hasting and Björn Ironside. Because of the earlier attacks, the Spanish coasts were now even more strongly defended and the Vikings were forced to sail through the Straits of Gibraltar into the Mediterranean where they plundered French and Italian towns.

Whilst on the Italian coast Hasting made an amusing and stupid mistake. The riches of the great city of Rome were legend, and he resolved to have them before returning from the campaign. His ships arrived near the walls of the city but, as they were obviously too strong to carry by assault, Hasting

A gold coin bearing the head of the Byzantine Emperor, Theophilus, of the kind brought back to Scandinavia by traders of Viking times

The "corpse" rises from the dead during Hasting's plan to capture "Rome"

worked out a cunning scheme. He sent some of his men to the gates of the city who shouted up to the guards that Hasting, their leader, had died a Christian, and they begged that he should be allowed Christian burial. The gates were opened and the bier, followed by a long procession of mourners, was carried into the city. Suddenly the 'corpse' leaped from the bier, the mourners pulled out weapons which they had concealed beneath their cloaks and the place was soon taken.

One can imagine Hasting's fury when he found that it was not Rome at all, but the comparatively small fishing town of Luna.

The fleet left the Mediterranean soon afterwards and sailed back to the French coast where it wintered in the Rhone delta. There were now far fewer ships, for the Spanish fleets had proved to be the most formidable they had met. In addition to the usual weapons, the Spanish ships carried two particularly lethal ones: the catapult, which hurled fiery bundles of oil-soaked cloth; and "Greek fire", a mixture of flaming naphtha and sulphur which was shot out of long tubes near the prow.

The stories they took back of the opposition they had met at sea stopped further Viking expeditions to Spain for more than a century, but when they began again none were as large as that of Hasting and Björn Ironside.

THE ATLANTIC VOYAGES

IT IS said that Naddod, a sea-rover, was driven off course and made a landfall at a large island. He landed, stayed there a while, then sailed back to his native Norway to tell of his find. He called it Snowland. One of his countrymen, Floke Vilgerdsson, went in search of the island hoping that it would be a good place in which to settle. But he arrived in a blizzard, the cattle he had taken with him had died during the winter through lack of fodder, and the spring was a long time coming. He sailed for home and was so disgusted with the place that he renamed it—Iceland.

Had the Vikings looked farther afield they would have found the island inhabited by a few monks who had gone there in search of solitude and peace. Later, when more Vikings arrived to settle, these early Christians moved out. They left behind them books, bells and croziers which reveal that they had originally come from Ireland. The men who took their place were from Norway, leaders of the first of the many who preferred to make a new home on forbidding Iceland rather than live under the harsh rule of Harald Fairhair, Norway's first king.

The Viking settlement of Iceland is known as The Land-taking and was completed between 870 and 930. A large number of farmers and fishermen, mainly from Norway but many from the Norse colonies in Britain, moved westwards to settle throughout the island.

Half a century later an even greater island was discovered. Living in Iceland at that time was Eirik the Red, a brave man but one very quick to anger. During a quarrel he killed two brothers and was outlawed for three years for manslaughter. Wondering where he should go during this time, he remembered an old tale that told of a strange land some 200 miles to the westward which had been sighted by some Vikings many years earlier but had never been revisited. Eirik followed their route across the Atlantic, heading West, and was amazed to see a vast land mass rising out of the mists of the Northern waters. He landed and spent most of his three years of exile on the island, thoroughly exploring the coastline, sailing up every fjord, naming the prominent capes and bays.

He was soon satisfied that it would be very suitable for settlement and, at the end of his years of exile, he returned to Iceland with his findings. Realising "that many would go there if it had a good name" he cleverly gave it the name of . . . Greenland.

His enthusiasm inspired others and in the spring of 986 he sailed back to the vast island with a fleet carrying nearly 700 men and women. Although eleven of the twenty-five ships foundered or turned back, the rest landed their would-be settlers. Under

Eirik's direction a colony was founded that was to grow in importance until the 14th century, when the 'Greenlanders' were almost exterminated by a massive invasion of Eskimos.

During the reign of Harald Fairhair, Norwegians settled in other islands. Some of these, in North British waters, were reached in the latter part of the 9th century. Here again, the quiet of the islands had attracted a few Irish hermits but they were soon ejected and the Norsemen went on to found an important colony there. The islands were particularly rich in sheep and therefore received the name of the "Faroe Islands"—Norse for "Sheep Islands".

Floke Vilgerdsson approaches the coast of Iceland

24

Other Norsemen settled on the Shetlands and Orkneys, and the Scottish Hebrides, all of which, indeed, were colonised before the Viking period began. In time these islands became completely Norwegian in language and culture, and the Norsemen did not regard them as foreign lands at all but as part of their own country. During Viking times they proved to be valuable bases from which to launch attacks upon Ireland and the Scottish mainland.

A New World

Bjarni Nerjolfsson, newly arrived in Greenland, had become an object of wonder and even contempt to the rest of his countrymen. He had intended to sail from Iceland to the new colony, had missed Greenland completely and after three days had come out of a bank of fog to see a range of long, low-lying islands ahead of his ship. Finally convinced that this place, whatever it was, was certainly not Greenland, he turned his ship's prow to the east and within four days made a safe landfall.

What none of the others could understand, experienced navigators that they were, was why the very incurious Bjarni had not landed and tried to find out something about this unknown country.

One of the men living in Greenland decided to do something about it. He was Leif Eiriksson, son of Eirik the Red, the founder of the colony. Leif hired Bjarni's boat and with thirty-five comrades, set off into the unknown. Most of the crew were like himself, tall, blue-

A fjord in the Faroe Islands today. Like Iceland, the solitary Faroes were an ideal refuge for monks and religious hermits for at least a hundred years before the Vikings arrived

eyed and fair-haired, but one was a surprising contrast to the rest. He was Tyrki, a short, dark-haired German who had known Leif from childhood.

The ship sailed about the year 1000 and at first followed a similar route to that of Bjarni but, when approaching the coast of the strange land, sailed in the opposite direction. The first land that was sighted, therefore, was the last that Bjarni had seen before turning homeward for Greenland. It proved to be a low, barren coast with high mountains in the distance that shone like glass in the pale autumn sunshine. Near the water's edge were thousands of flat, circular stones which caused Leif to name the place 'Helluland' from *hellur*, or stone. He went ashore in a boat, thus becoming the first known European to set foot on the shores of the New World, for the place where he landed was, centuries later, to become Frobisher Bay, North Canada.

Travelling southwards, more land was sighted. It was well wooded with long stretches of white sand. Leif again went ashore and called it 'Markland' meaning forest land. It is believed that this was Cape Porcupine, Labrador. Two days later they sighted the large land mass of Cape Cod and continued to move slowly along the coast "having a north-east wind, and were two days at sea before they saw land. They steered toward it and touched the island lying before the north part of the land. When they went on land they surveyed it, for by good fortune the weather was serene. They found the grass sprinkled with dew, and it happened by chance that they touched the dew with their hands and perceived that it had a sweet taste which they had not before noticed. Then they returned to the ship and sailed through a bay lying between the island and a tongue of land running toward the north . . . They went ashore at a place where a river flowed out from a lake . . . Afterwards they held a consultation and resolved to remain at this place during the winter. Then they erected large buildings. . . ."

During their stay Tyrki was missing for several days. When a search party found him he was babbling happily in his own language and rolling his eyes. He had been drinking the juice of over-ripe grapes and was intoxicated. Because of this incident the place was called 'Vinland'. It was probably what we know today as New England.

Finally the time came for Leif and his men to leave this exciting new world and return to Greenland where the story of their adventures were to form part of the great *Graenlendinga* (or

Greenland) Saga. That winter brought a great deal of sickness to the island, amongst the many who died being Eirik the Red. Leif settled down on his father's estate and lived, as the chronicler wrote, "full of riches and honour", and known to all as Leif the Lucky.

Return to the New World

Leif's brother, Thorvald, also hired Bjarni's lucky boat and sailed to Vin-

Above: this statue of Leif Eiriksson stands today in Reykjavik, the capital of Iceland. It was presented to the Icelanders by the United States of America. Left: Leif comes ashore at 'Helluland'

land. He wintered there, using the same huts that Leif had built during his previous stay. He and his men explored the country and found it rich and beautiful. On reaching a particularly lovely promontory Thorvald exclaimed, "Here I will establish my farm".

Soon afterwards, however, his party was attacked by a group of lean and ugly men with lank, stringy black hair, big eyes and wide cheekbones. They were the natives who lived nearby, whom the Vikings were to call *Skraelings*, and to whom Columbus, nearly

The rocky coastline of Hebron, North Labrador, which would have been sighted by the early Viking explorers on their way south from Greenland to "Markland" (South Labrador)

five centuries later, was to give the name "Indians".

Thorvald was struck by an arrow and died soon afterwards, being buried, at his request, on the promontory he liked so much. Crosses were placed at the head and foot of his grave, for, like his brother Leif, he had been baptised as a Christian.

In the year 1020 the most ambitious expedition so far left for Vinland. It was led by Thorfinn Karlsefni, an Icelander, who commanded three ships which carried a large number of settlers. Amongst them were two unusual people —a short red-haired man and woman— wearing clothes that differed from those of the Vikings. They were actually Naki and his wife Haekia, two "kilted highlanders" from Scotland, who were to act as scouts, for they were both 'as fleet as deer'.

The expedition reached Vinland and the two Britons were sent ashore with orders to explore the territory and return after two days. When they did so they carried half-ripe grapes and self-sown grain. The latter was probably wild maize. Winter was approaching and the Vikings were glad of the huts which Leif had built and which still stood firm after twenty years. It was a mild winter and the cattle were able to be left out, finding plenty of forage. There was less food for the humans, however, and they were soon nearly starving. A whale stranded on the beach only made them ill when they tried to eat its flesh.

Spring came at last, bringing the *Skraelings* with it. At first the natives were friendly, wishing to trade pelts and skins for pieces of woven cloth. Although the Vikings' stock of this material grew steadily smaller, the trading continued without incident until an ox belonging to Karlsefni came bellowing out of a wood, frightening the natives. They believed this to be an omen of ill-luck and ran off. A few days later scores of skin boats arrived, packed with *Skraelings*, armed and ready for war.

But the Vikings were ready with their

swords and axes of iron—a metal unknown to their enemies—and although men fell on both sides, the natives finally fled to their boats and frantically paddled away. Although the battle had been won, Karlsefni was forced to give up the idea of colonisation. There were not enough of them to be constantly at war with the *Skraelings*, they could not expect reinforcements from Greenland, and Norway was too far away.

Before they returned to Greenland, however, Karlsefni's wife gave birth to a son. He was called Snorri—the first European to be born in the New World.

Other parties later went to Vinland and to the well-wooded Markland but they always were too few and the natives too many. Had they succeeded in turning Leif's discovery into a Scandinavian colony, how different the history of the world might have been!

The Viking's weapons were a sharp contrast to those of the primitive Red Indian. "Skraeling", the name given to the Red Indian by the Vikings, means, appropriately, "screecher"

THE STRUGGLE FOR ENGLAND

ENGLAND WAS facing difficult times. Her coasts were under constant attack from Danish fleets, some composed of nearly a hundred vessels, and the small garrisons scattered in forts along the shore were helpless to stop them. In desperation, the king of the English, Aethelred, later to be called the 'Unready', or 'Redeless'—meaning lacking in counsel—bribed the Vikings to go away. In 991 he gave them 10,000 pounds of silver as Danegeld, three years later another 16,000 pounds, and in 1002, the vast sum of 24,000 pounds of silver.

Although many of the Vikings left the country, a large number remained to join others who were peacefully living as farmers and traders. Then Aethelred in a moment of madness ordered every Dane to be killed on St. Brice's Day, November 13th, 1002. Amongst those slaughtered was the sister of Denmark's king, Sven Forkbeard, who, on hearing the tragic news, immediately called up his men and ordered every available ship to the attack. Sven landed without opposition and went on to conquer nearly all England.

Sven had to return to Denmark but new reinforcements arrived. They were commanded by Thorkel the Tall who, in 1012, raised the Danegeld to 48,000 pounds. With this he paid off most of his men whilst he, with forty-five ships of his own, remained as a mercenary in Aethelred's service, with his headquarters in London.

Sven then returned to England to take command of the Viking forces, but this time he resolved to conquer the country and remain as its king. His army marched swiftly inland and soon only London and the West remained unconquered. Aethelred fled to the court of Richard of Normandy and Thorkel, finding himself deserted by the king, opened the gates of London and the Danish army poured in. Sven Forkbeard was now nominally the ruler of the whole of England, but he died soon afterwards.

The Anglo-Saxon nobles immediately sent to Aethelred and begged him to return and lead them against the Danes. He did so, bringing with him an important ally, Olaf, later King of Norway, and an army of Norsemen.

The combined fleet of Saxon and

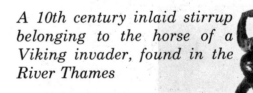

A 10th century inlaid stirrup belonging to the horse of a Viking invader, found in the River Thames

Norse ships rowed up the Thames to attack London but when it drew near London Bridge it came under a fierce bombardment of stones from the bridge and a crossfire of arrows and spears from either bank. The ships pulled back, but only long enough to allow their crews to build protective roofs made from thatch torn from nearby cottages. Now not only did the stones rebound harmlessly from the roofs, but some of the attackers slipped into the water and tied ropes from their ships to the piers supporting the bridge. The ships then went backwards and the bridge, already heavy with armed men and piles of stones, gave way. The centre collapsed, spilling many of the Danes into the river, and the rest soon dispersed.

London was captured and the Danes sued for peace. This battle was recounted later by the Scandinavians as part of a saga, and formed the basis of our familiar nursery rhyme. The stirring original began:

London Bridge is broken down,
Gold is won and bright renown,
Shields resounding, war horns
                    sounding,
Hildar shouting in the din.
Arrows singing, mailcoats ringing
Odin makes our Olaf win!

The Great King Knut

Sven Forkbeard had a younger son, Knut. Aethelred also had a son, Edmund Ironside. Like their fathers, they were rivals and fought each other for a great prize—the kingdom of England. At first, Edmund seemed the more fortunate. Sven died suddenly, Aethelred came back to England, and Knut was driven out of the country.

He returned in 1015 with his brother Harald and a large fleet, determined to win back the country which had so nearly been his father's. He led his army through the southern shires and, having forced Wessex to submit, he advanced into Mercia. Meanwhile, Edmund and his two allies, Eadric of Mercia and Uhtred of Northumbria were in the north, attacking and plundering where men refused to support their cause. It seemed as if both sides were intent on a campaign of murder and looting, with little regard for the country as a whole. Then Uhtred, learning that Knut had reached York, deserted Edmund and swore allegiance to his former enemy. This encouraged Knut to march South to attack London where the old king, Aethelred, lay dying.

As he drew up his forces for the assault, news was brought to him—the king was dead. With the unfortunate 'Unready's' death, there ended a disastrous reign of thirty-eight years. The Witangemot—or Parliament— immediately elected Edmund to be king in his stead.

Ignoring this news, Knut pressed on with his plans, cutting a deep channel along the right bank of the Thames in order that his ships might pass to the west of the city without having to attack the heavily defended bridge. Once this was done, he was able to assail the city from both sides. He sent envoys to the city gates, bearing his threat to destroy London unless a

The marriage ceremony between Knut and Emma of Normandy

great ransom was paid and Edmund—who was behind the city walls—was handed over to him. Even as his men gave their message, however, Edmund slipped away during the night, reached Wessex, and soon had an army flocking to his banner.

Knut marched his own army to the south-west and a series of battles were fought. In the last of these, at Assundune in Essex, although the Saxons were greatly outnumbered, they seemed for a time to be steadily gaining the advantage. At the critical moment, however, Eadric fled from the field with his forces. As a result, Edmund met with a crushing defeat. The losses were so terrible that both sides thankfully signed a peace treaty. Edmund was to rule Wessex, and Knut the rest of England, including the still defiant London.

A few months later, however, Edmund died. No rival could now challenge Knut, who made his position even stronger by marrying Emma of Normandy, Aethelred's widow. Yet even if a rival had come forward, he would have had little support for by now everyone was weary of fighting and bloodshed and anxious to acclaim a strong man who could bring peace and prosperity to a battle-torn land.

The young Knut, who was still only about twenty, was crowned early in 1017 and given the title *Rex Angliae*, king of England. A Dane now sat on the throne; the Saxon dynasty was at an end. Fortunately the new king was to prove to be one who ruled the country well and wisely. He was later to become king of Denmark, of Norway and overlord of Scotland. As a ruler of these kingdoms, but more especially for his wise and prosperous reign, Knut has become familiar in history as—Canute the Great.

THE BEAUTIFUL ART OF THE VIKING AGE

IN PRE-VIKING times, the old Norse artists reached a very high standard of craftsmanship. They used many subjects in their designs but mostly favoured curving and twisting animals. By about 800, however, it seemed as if they had reached the limit of their skill; there was nothing new to be done. Then, with the invention of an entirely new animal, their art took on a new lease of life. This was a strange, mythical creature composed of many real ones—lions, bears, dogs and so on —which was used over and over again, and which has become known as the Oseberg or "gripping beast".

These composite creatures are very typical of the art of the first half of the Viking era. They are fat little animals with large solemn eyes and plump little faces. They sprawl inside the edge of the design, apparently fighting for space, hanging on to each other with clutching claws, clambering upwards, crisscrossing over and under each other until the whole area of the design is full of twisted, contorted movement. These "gripping beasts" were used in an amazing variety of objects—on jewellery, armour, ships, beds, roofposts, sledges, wagons and so on.

As the Viking raids went on, so men returned with works of art from other countries although a great deal of valuable objects also flowed into Scandinavia through normal trade. Most of these works came from England, Ireland and the country of the Franks and some came from the Middle East. The Nordic artists studied this foreign material, adapting some of the styles into their own work.

By the 10th century, the 'gripping beasts' had been replaced by the animal forms of the 'Jelling' style, the name Jelling being taken from the royal burial chamber at Jelling in central Jutland in Denmark where the style was first discovered. The Jelling style featured long, ribbon-like animals, which were often lions intertwined with snakes, and was carried on in the

A 10th century silver amulet in the form of a crucifix found at Birka, Sweden

11th century, being found in church carvings, or jewellery and inscribed on natural stones.

Carving pictures and words on such natural stones, indeed, was quite common in the Viking Age. The stones were called 'rune-stones', and were usually memorial slabs. Some merely bear inscriptions in an ancient alphabet of sixteen characters, one that was used in England, too, before being replaced by the Roman alphabet. Others are

The "gripping beast". This one is engraved on a brooch found in Jutland, Denmark

with a snake and a representation of Christ.

Another example is the Lärbro stone. This shows a Viking longship with its crew armed and ready, with the steersman standing at the oar at the stern, whilst it proudly thrusts through the waves, its square sail bellying before a strong wind. Above the ships are shown scenes of a fierce battle, and a rider—obviously the warrior for whom the stone was carved—arriving at the gates of Valhalla.

Artists of the Viking Age also produced a large quantity of carved figures although they were nearly all quite small, Thor and Frey being the two most popular subjects. A large number of figures of court officials and men on

The great stone at Jelling, in Denmark, raised in the 10th century by King Harold Bluetooth

carved with a wide variety of scenes, and some show both words and pictures. One fine example is the great triangular-shaped boulder set up at Jelling as a memorial stone by King Harold Bluetooth. As well as an inscription in ancient lettering in memory both of his parents and of Harold's own deeds, the stone bears pictures of a large mythical beast locked together

A silver bowl from Gotland, Sweden, showing the ribbon-shaped Jelling design round the rim

horseback have been found, many of which are possibly chessmen.

The Craftsmen

From what has been discovered in ship burials, other graves and in churches it is very obvious that the men of the Viking Age were brilliant craftsmen.

The smith was the aristocrat of them all, for every warrior's life depended upon his workmanship and the product of a smith—a good sword or axe—was something to be treasured and passed on. The great god Thor carried a hammer, the symbol of the smith, and many swords were believed to have magic properties. The smith's trade brought him prestige and wealth and some of the richest graves that have been excavated in Scandinavia are those of smiths. Obviously, they intended to carry on their work after death for

many were buried with the tools of their trade. In one grave alone, in Biggland, Norway, four swords, four spearheads, seven axes, two shield bosses and nine knives were found buried with an anvil, hammer and a complete collection of smith's tools.

Some smiths preferred to work with precious metals, and here their craftsmanship has rarely been surpassed. Rings, brooches, amulets, neck-rings and other personal jewellery are of a very high standard as are their caskets, spurs, mounts and similar articles.

The Scandinavian countries were rich in forests, the wood from which was used by carpenters to produce some truly magnificent work. The examples of the carpenter's art found at the Oseberg burial are probably the finest known. Even more noteworthy than the intricately carved prow and stern of the ship are the beautifully poised and finely inworked animal head posts,

The craftsman who forged this sword was skilled indeed, for it had magical powers: wielded by its owner, Sigurd, a legendary Viking hero, it could split a stone anvil with one blow (see 'Arms and Armour', page 64). With its aid, Sigurd is said to have slain several monsters, including a giant snake named Fafnir that inhabited the mountain-tops of Norway

Left: reconstruction of a smith's grave. He is surrounded by his tools and some of his finished work (swords and spearheads). In the same tradition, horses were often buried with their dead warrior masters. Right: a carved wooden horse's head, one of many unearthed at Gokstad, Sweden, from a Viking ship burial

probably used in religious ceremonies, found on the deck.

The dead Queen's personal possessions clearly show the pleasure derived from treasures created by imaginative artists. Figures have been carved in relief in oak, maple and beech and the design accentuated by means of metal fittings and silver nails.

Houses were also beautifully carved, edgeboards particularly being decorated with twisted dragon's tails and the ends projecting over the eaves of the house shaped like the heads of dragons. Door frames, too, were elaborately carved and within the house the beds, benches, chair-backs and chests were richly inworked with animals and

Above: an armlet of twisted silver found in Russia on one of the former Norse trading routes. Right: an elaborate ceremonial cart of oak and beech found in a Viking ship buried at Oseberg, in Norway. On the front and sides are carved intertwining animal figures

the figures of gods and goddesses.

The craftsmen worked in other materials too. Amber was used for jewellery, reindeer antlers and walrus ivory for a variety of pins, combs and playing pieces, whilst soapstone, a conveniently fireproof mineral, was widely used for cooking utensils, moulds, crucibles and so on.

At first, little pottery was produced in Scandinavia as most was imported from the Rhineland. Tableware and other vessels were more commonly made from wood. It was not until late in the Viking period that pottery was produced in any quantity.

Thus, the Viking Age was not only marked by its war-like spirit, but by its art and culture as well.

Above, left: an amulet in the shape of Thor's hammer, from Sweden, an outstanding example of the goldsmith's craft. Below: a gilt-bronze weather-vane which originally decorated the prow of a Viking ship

LIFE IN THE HOMELAND

The King and his People

A king of France, who wished to make a treaty with the Vikings, told their messengers to bid their master come and stand before him. The reply was short and to the point. "We know no master. All of us are equal!"

This may have been true when the warriors were a-viking, but it was not so at other times. In the halls of the rich and powerful, the lord and his family sat in the place of honour—the "high seats"; others were in the "low seats"

Reconstruction of a pair of drinking horns bearing silver-gilt foil mounts. The horn raised by the chieftain (opposite) was very similar

BRITISH MUSEUM

whilst the lowly sat by the door, often not on seats at all but on the floor!

At the top of the social tree were the "high born". These were the jarls or earls, noblemen who owned lands, goods, their own ships and their own small army of retainers (or housecarls). The jarls elected the king, but if he proved unsatisfactory he could be deposed and another elected in his place. In time of war the king—or the battle leader chosen by the king—demanded absolute obedience. He was also expected to be more courageous than his followers and to be an example to them in battle. He had to have the ability to inspire them with a word or a joke when things were not going well, and was expected to be generous, giving his men gifts of weapons, clothes, jewellery and drink as a token of his recognition of their courage.

The backbone of the Scandinavian races in Viking times, however, were that class of the community equivalent to the yeomen of Anglo-Saxon times who owned a little land and were independent. Many of these became traders too, and, as such, rich and powerful.

There was also a large class of freedmen, semi-skilled labourers and craftsmen who, for the most part, worked for others.

Thralls, or slaves, had been known in Scandinavia from earliest times. During the Viking period, however, their numbers greatly increased, many being Slavs, whom the Vikings had captured in their raids round the Baltic and in Russia. Generally they suffered hard, unending toil, a writer of the

A Scandinavian chieftain, his wife and "jarls", feast at the "high seat"

times stating that no man "deigned to put his hand to a flail, or any other labour on earth; nor did a woman deign to put her hands to the grinding of a quern, or to knead a cake, or to wash her clothes, but had a foreign man or woman to work for them".

Even so, a slave's life was not without hope. In both Norway and Sweden it was possible for a slave to earn money with which to buy his freedom, and even to win it in battle, by beating off and killing the enemy by his master's side.

Food and Drink

The clean fresh air of the north and the appetite that comes from hunting, fishing and work in the open air meant that the kitchen was a very busy place in Viking times. There was a variety of dishes to prepare and the housewife, or the nobleman's cooks, must have been kept hard at work for most of the day.

The cooking vessels were made of iron or of a fireproof substance called soapstone and were similar to those found in modern kitchens—pots, pans, frying pans and ladles—together with cauldrons and spits. Meat was roasted on a spit, the Norse word for which is *steikja*, from which comes the English word 'steak'. Meat was also boiled, pork and veal being particularly popular. The selection varied in various parts of Scandinavia but farms and hunting provided everything that was needed. Adam of Bremen, a German historian who wrote in the latter half

also became part of the menu. Small game—geese, chickens and hares—were also popular.

Bread was made from barley or rye and there was plenty of butter and cheese. There was also a kind of porridge made from barley-meal. It was eaten with wooden, horn or bone spoons; knives were used to cut up the meat and spread the butter, but there were no forks. No doubt fingers were used for most things.

A meal in progress in a wealthy merchant's household

of the 11th century, stated: "They manage to live off their livestock, using the milk for food and their wool for clothing. Consequently their country breeds many brave warriors who attack more than they are themselves attacked for they have not been softened by rich harvests..."

Whatever Adam may have believed, the people of this time lived well, eating sheep, calves and pigs, goats, oxen and horses. In parts of Norway and in Iceland, polar bears, seal and whales

The meals were made more interesting with vegetables, cabbage, beans, peas, garlic and onions; for dessert there were berries and nuts and apples were found in a barrel in the Oseberg burial chamber. The whole meal was washed down with a drink called *Skyr,* which was milk curdled and separated from the whey. It is amusing to picture a tough old Viking seated at his family table eating bread and cheese and washing it down with milk!

But a great deal of strong drink—ale,

bear and mead—was also drunk. In the large household it was taken round to the diners by servants known as pourers *(skenkjarar)* who filled the drinking horns from a large container. In the royal households and in the homes of the rich, imported wine was also very popular.

Unlike other European nations of the time, the Scandinavians, and especially the Norsemen and Icelanders, were particular about their personal cleanliness. In a famous poem, the *Hávamál,* which is full of advice on life and living, it tells of a guest being greeted at the table "with water, a towel and a hearty welcome".

The *Hávamál* also says: "Beer is not so good for men as it is said to be; the more a man drinks the less control he has of his thoughts."

How many of the old Vikings, one wonders, took notice of this wise advice!

Cooking utensils. Top: an iron cauldron hanging from a tripod for cooking out of doors. When used inside, this cauldron would have been suspended from the roof by the large hook (see page 42). The other vessels are soapstone pots. As well as being boiled and roasted, meat was sometimes placed in a shallow pit, covered with hot embers, sealed with earth and baked

Houses

A familiar type of house in Viking times was a rectangular building with its longer walls curved in at each end. This was a relic, it is believed, of the days when roofs of houses were made from upturned boats. Even when boats were no longer used, the familiar shape still persisted.

Another type was the long- or hall-house, with straight sides. Such houses were nearly always of timber planking sometimes with alternating layers of turf for warmth.

A great deal is known about these old houses because of extensive excavations which have not only uncovered their foundations but also household and other articles. One such excavation indeed, is reminiscent of Pompeii. At about 1104 in Iceland, the volcano of Hekla erupted and covered a score or so of 10th century farms with a deep layer of ash. Their digging brought to light not only the houses and farm

The interior of a typical wood-built house, showing the stone-lined hearth used for cooking and the sleeping areas along the walls. The mattresses were stuffed with straw or hay and often covered with sheepskin

or wattle-and-daub. Sometimes only the roof supports were of wood, the walls and even the roof being made of turf which was found to be warmer than wood in winter. The turf style of building was taken by the Vikings to Iceland and then to Greenland, where, in any case, there was little suitable stone or timber. In the Orkneys, Shetlands and Faroes stone was abundant and the houses were built of this material,

buildings but also the farming implements, furniture and so on, of the time.

Another excavation at Stöng in Iceland has revealed a complete farm that is typical of Viking times. The main house was built of turves laid upon stone courses. It had a main hall measuring 12.25 by 5.85 metres. Along its walls were benches of earth enclosed by wooden panelling and supported by upright posts. These served as seats

42

during the day and beds at night. The main living room which led off this hall also had benches along the walls. Both rooms had a central fireplace. Smaller rooms, including the kitchen, were under the same roof, whilst a number of outbuildings were sited nearby.

An even larger farm complex had been excavated in the Shetlands which was given the romantic name of Jarl-

modern sauna, which must have been a welcome luxury to the owner and his sons on their return from a long voyage on a crowded longship! Around the settlement was a series of walls, some built by the Viking owner, others by Picts who occupied the site long before the Vikings landed.

Below, left: building with wattle and daub (interlacing twigs, or straw, and mud). This house, built as it was almost entirely of wood, was typical of 10th century Denmark. In the bleaker island colonies such as Greenland, houses were built more solidly from earth, stones and turf

shof by Sir Walter Scott. It is particularly interesting because it represents a settlement which has been gradually extended over the centuries: it began simply as one long-house, made up of one room and a small kitchen; later generations added a second long-house, a house for their Pict slaves who helped on the farm, stables, byres, barns, and a smithy. They even built a bath-house, complete with steam-bath, rather like a

Country Life

When they were not "a-viking", many of the Scandinavians were excellent farmers. Their year began in the spring when the snow had gone and the cattle could be brought out from the byres where they had spent the winter to graze on the new tender grass. The first big task was the spring ploughing. This was done with wooden ploughs drawn

Spinning and weaving in 10th century Iceland: an iron comb was drawn through the wool before spinning. The red dye was taken from the madder plant, and the weights at the bottom of the weaving frame were made of soapstone or baked clay

by oxen with one man guiding the plough and another walking beside the animals ready to encourage them with a stick if they became lazy.

There was also wood to be cut and peat to be dug, walls and fences to be built or repaired after the fierce winds and heavy snow of the winter months, new barns to be erected and fields to be manured. There was the sowing of oats, barley, and occasionally wheat,

and some vegetables, too, were cultivated.

When this work was over many of the men, especially the younger ones who were eager for excitement and for wealth that could be won only by raiding and not from inheritance, would join a band of Vikings and set off in the longships. Overnight, it would seem, they changed from hard-working, diligent farmers, happy with their children or their families, into crazed, blood-thirsty pirates, or so the old Saxon monks who wrote of their exploits would have us believe. Today, scholars are inclined to dismiss a great deal of what was written about the Vikings as having stemmed from fear, hate and ignorance.

Even when the Vikings had gone from the farms, there was still much to do. In the summer the young lambs had to be cared for and the sheep sheared. The women were especially busy: in addition to the daily milking they had to prepare and salt food for the winter. One of the important foodstuffs they made was a long-lasting butter from sour cream, which, when placed in a cool, underground room would keep for months, especially when packed in ice and salt. Cheese was kept fresh in the same way.

The Vikings returned at harvest-time, after which further stocks of food for the humans and fodder for the animals were collected and stored. When the first snows of winter fell, this was the signal for indoor activities to begin. There were hides and skins

Building a barn with wattle and daub

to be dressed and made into clothing, belts and harness, tools and furniture to be made, boats to be repaired and made ready for the spring. The women and girls, meanwhile, would be busy weaving cloth, spinning wool, and doing needlework and embroidery.

When the weather allowed, the men would go hunting and fishing. In those days the rivers were full of salmon and trout, the forests and mountains well-stocked with boars, deer, elk, bears and, in the northern regions, vast herds of reindeer. The men travelled on skis, often pulling their kill on sleighs behind them. In the evenings the families would gather near a cheery fire of pine logs to sing, tell stories or play chess and other games.

And so the winter passed pleasantly enough until the snow melted before spring and it was time for those who who chose to go a-viking once more.

Town Life

Originally, in Scandinavia, there were only villages, small settlements and scattered farms. Then, during Viking times, as the countries became wealthy

Ploughing: a time of peace between Viking seasons

A bone dice holder and play counters, all of Viking origin

from trade and from raiding, towns appeared. Many of these sprang up along the coasts of the North Sea and the Baltic. Today, few remain. The rest have vanished, leaving only a few tumbled stones or grass covered mounds where once there was colourful, bustling life.

These towns had streets of wooden houses, some with vertical planking, others with wattle-and-daub panels between the main timbers. The gable ends of the house faced well-paved streets and had barns and stables at the rear. There were also districts in these towns where the craftsmen lived and carried out their trade—the iron-workers, glass-makers, carpenters, potters and so on. All of these towns were beside water, usually a fjord which gave access to the open sea, and with gently sloping beaches where the boats could unload their cargoes. There were also rows of boat-houses at the water's edge where the ships could be secured during the winter months.

In every town there was always one house larger than the rest. This was the home of the jarl of the city or even the king himself. It was large because of the importance of the owner and because it had to accommodate the house-carls and all the others in the lord's service, together with visiting noblemen and their retinues. All these had to be fed and the kitchens often formed a large part of the building. There were also large outbuildings nearby to house the hundreds of thralls owned by the jarl and his family.

The central part of the house was the great hall. Here was the "highseat" where the jarl sat with his family, his councillors and his favoured warriors. All others sat at tables lower down the hall.

Below: a king, armed with sword, from a set of Viking chessmen. Right: other pieces include a queen, a knight, a bishop and pawns

There were two meals a day: the first, or 'day meal' was served early in the morning, and the 'night meal', which was the main meal of the day, in the evening.

Men in Viking times were great drinkers. They drank beer and ale and mead made from honey, sometimes flavoured with herbs. Drinking horns were used, most of which were made from cattle horns, and which were often beautifully carved and decorated with gold or silver mountings. The meal would end at a sign from the lord and it is told of one king, Harald Hardrada, who was somewhat mean, that he would rap on the table as soon as he had had enough so that the tables would be cleared by his servants. Many of those present, if they had been late in being served, remained hungry!

The evening would end with a performance by one or more skalds, the poets and minstrels of the day. They kept alive the stories of heroes and battles which, when later put into prose as sagas, became the main source of Viking history.

Not every home had such feasting and drinking. Many families in those days preferred to spend their evenings quietly in their homes dicing or playing various board games. They were very fond of these, particularly chess, which came to Scandinavia via the Arabs who in turn brought it from India. A kind of draughts and a game called "fox-and-geese" were also popular.

Costume and Ornament

The popular idea of a Viking warrior as a great bearded ox of a man, wearing a huge horned helmet, his body smothered in shapeless fur, is not a very well-founded one. The men, and women, of the Viking Age loved colour and magnificence and their dress was more refined and elegant than is commonly supposed.

The nobleman or warrior first put on a linen or fine wool shirt and long, tight-fitting underpants; on top of this went a kirtle-type, tailored garment reaching from his shoulders to mid-thigh, or

A plaited armlet, from a hoard of Viking silver found in Orkney. Among other pieces were necklets and bracelets

lower, fitting snugly at the waist and with tight fitting sleeves. This kirtle was worn in many different colours—green and scarlet being the favourites—and often decorated with gold or silver thread embroidery.

His breeches varied in style. Some were ankle-length and close-fitting; others were wide and baggy and gathered in at the knee, rather like 'plus fours'.

On top of everything he wore a cloak, sometimes made of highly coloured cloth with a decorative border, sometimes from pelts of beaver, sable, fox or marten. These cloaks were fastened by an ornate pin or clasp.

His headgear was a tight-fitting cap, a tall "Russian" style hat, pointed or round topped, or one with a broad floppy brim. His belt was also richly decorated, was clasped about his waist by a silver or bronze buckle and supported his purse and a knife. Shoes were made from leather and were, in appearance, somewhat like moccasins. During bad weather he wore boots made from untanned cow's skin. He also wore gloves or mittens.

On special occasions, the king or nobleman would wear a splendid trailing robe made of imported silk. With his metal collar and silver or gold arm bangles he must have looked a very imposing person.

The Vikings were fussy about their appearance also, to judge by the number of combs that have been found in their graves. Their moustaches and beards were neatly trimmed, their hair cut fairly short, sometimes with a fringe that came to their eyebrows.

The women were equally well dressed. They wore a long robe falling to the ground at the front, but longer at the back so that it trailed behind. Some were made from silk or satin imported from Spain and the Orient. They always wore two oval brooches, now called 'tortoise' from their shape. These were worn almost as high as the shoulder-blades and were often joined by festoons of glass and amber beads to another, central brooch. There were many

The remains of an elaborate bone comb of the Viking Age

other brooches, bracelets and rings.

A belt spanned the waist from which hung a variety of household objects— keys, a comb, scissors and needle cases, a purse and so on. Married women wore their hair gathered into a knot at the back and concealed by a head-dress, unmarried girls wore theirs loose and flowing. Cloaks similar to those of the men were also worn. An embroidered tapestry from the Oseberg burial shows that the girls wore 'freer' clothes. One is shown wearing a short dress and knee-length boots!

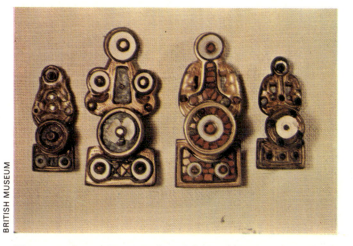

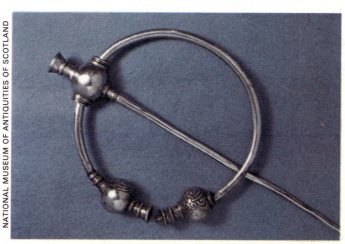

Two contrasting styles of craftsmanship in jewellery. Above, left: elaborate bronze disc-on-bow brooches from Gotland, Sweden. Right: a late 10th century silver brooch from the same hoard as the armlet (opposite), with ends sculpted in the shape of thistles. Below: glass beads, originally brought to Scandinavia from far-off lands, found at the ancient trading centre of Birka, in Sweden, in the graves of Viking womenfolk

Trade and Barter

Because of the activities of the Vikings, a great part of the world was opened to trade. Their ships sailed to Iceland, Greenland and Britain, to Russia, France, Spain and the Mediterranean, to Constantinople, Byzantium and other great cities of the Middle East and goods poured back to Scandinavia to be sold or resold. They included shiploads of sea ivory and walrus hides; slaves, furs and feathers; cloth, glass, pottery, wine, and sword-blades, silks, spices, brocades and delicate jewellery; they were bound for towns specially built for this purpose, for the Viking Age produced something quite new—the market town of the professional merchant and trader.

Typical of several large trading centres was Hedeby in the South of Denmark, on the banks of the Treene

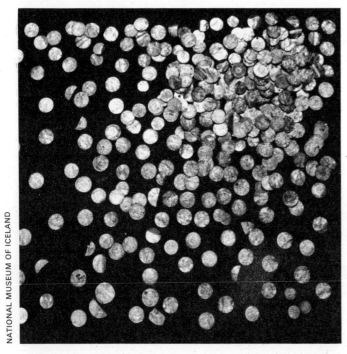

A hoard of coins from many countries which have found their way to Iceland through the far-flung trading connections of the Vikings. Among them are the half and quarter pieces used for trading in smaller sums

which links the Eider with the North Sea. Excavations began on the site in 1900 and have revealed many of the reasons for its former importance.

By the 10th century, Hedeby covered an area of some sixty acres, enclosed on three sides by a great semi-circular rampart. The principal part of the city was a large space which served as a huge open-air market. Wares from all over Europe, from the East and from the Atlantic Islands were displayed on stalls or laid out on the ground during the day. At night, all this wealth was put away and guarded by traders, ships' crews and others, who lived in tents and shacks spread around three sides of the market area. The fourth side was the water's edge where scores of merchant ships lay at their moorings or were hauled up on to the beach.

Behind this market lay the city where the merchants lived in well laid out streets. The foundations of the houses that formed these streets have been found in a well-preserved condition. There were also areas in the city specially built for the local craftsmen and workmen.

Goods were brought by ships coming in the Eider; they were then taken by carts to Hedeby where they were sold or placed in other ships to be carried onwards to the Baltic.

Hedeby, like other market towns, handled internal as well as external trade. Locally made goods came to be sold there, although many of them, especially soapstone pots and jewellery, were also taken from settlement to settlement and to remote farmhouses by the travelling pedlars and tinkers of the time. Most of the buying and selling was by barter, although silver coins gradually came into use. At first, they were not used as currency but were valued by their weight. Many coins have been found that had been cut into halves and quarters for smaller sums, and scales and a set of weights must have been a vital part of the trader's equipment.

Many Arabic and Byzantine coins have been found throughout the Scandinavian countries, mostly dating from the 9th and 10th centuries. In the latter part of the 10th and for much of the 11th century, the coins are mainly English. Some were the result of trade; many more must have been part of the Danegeld brought back by warriors returning from England.

However they were obtained, they represented great wealth. No wonder that the Viking Period is also called the Silver Age of Scandinavia!

NATIONAL MUSEUM OF IRELAND

Above: dating from the Viking occupation of Ireland, these tinned bronze scales were found in 1866 at Islandbridge, Dublin, when workmen were making a deep cutting for a new railway line

Below: on the waterfront at Hedeby, Denmark, a trader displays rich fabrics from the Eastern Mediterranean

Sports and Pastimes

For the men of the Viking Age, life was not all work and fighting; they got a great deal of fun out of life. Being so strong and courageous themselves, they naturally enjoyed strenuous outdoor pastimes and their audiences derived as much pleasure from them as the contestants.

Wrestling was a favourite sport: in one version the opponents wrestled in a lake or fjord. The aim was to see who could keep the other's head below water for the longest time! Running, jumping, skiing and skating, too, were popular sports in their season and men vied with each other in military pastimes such as fencing, archery and spear-throwing.

They also played a game with bats and balls but the rules have unfor-

An unusual watersport: wrestling in a fjord

tunately been lost. All that is known is that it had to be played on a smooth, level surface and usually in winter.

There was also bareback racing on horses in which the riders used their whips on their rivals as well as on their mounts, a sport which often became very wild and dangerous indeed. Horses were also trained to fight each other and, in Iceland especially, such contests frequently ended with the owners fighting each other!

There were many ways in which the long winter evenings were spent. In addition to board games, chess, draughts and so on, there was dancing, either singly or in groups. Nothing is known about the music of the time but harps were common and there were pipes and fiddles to accompany the singing and dancing.

One of the greatest pleasures, however, lay in the spoken word. Poetry was composed and recited and there were a number of word games similar to those played at parties today. In the evening the family would gather about the pine-log fire and whilst the blizzard raged outside shaking the timber shingles, or snow fell to cover the countryside, one of their number would retell the stories that reached back to the beginning of time.

The children would sit wide-eyed, whilst they listened to stories of the mountain dwarfs who only emerged at night, for sunlight was fatal to them. They heard of the strange race called trolls, of the cunning elves and of the huge, shaggy giants, Thor's enemies, who used trees as clubs and tossed boulders about as if they were stones.

They never tired of the stories of the swan maidens who flew to some quiet mountain lake where they doffed their feather dresses to become, for a while, maidens in human form; and of Volund who, seeing three such maidens, hid their dresses and would not return them until one of them promised to be his wife.

Then, after the tale-telling was done, and after a drink of hot milk or warmed ale against the chill night air, it was time for bed.

Great Occasions

Three great festivals were held every year throughout Scandinavia in Viking times. One was held about the middle of October, "to greet the winter", another at mid-winter called Jól, and a spring celebration in the middle of April, "to greet the summer". The most important of these was Jól.

After the long, dark winter, the first glimpse of the sun in the Northern latitudes was a time for rejoicing and Jól often lasted as long as two weeks. It was very much a family festival and it was believed that dead relatives came back to celebrate with the living.

The long nights encouraged ghosts to wander abroad and visit their kin, and it was necessary to make them welcome and thus earn their goodwill. A table loaded with food and drink was prepared for the visitors from "outside", beds were made ready and fires heaped with logs to warm their icy bodies, for many were newly risen from dark and damp burial places whilst others came soaked and dripping from the sea.

There was also a belief that each house was visited at Jól-tide by an elf or goblin with a long white beard and a jaunty red cap. This little fellow was the forerunner of our present-day Santa Claus.

Originally, Jól was held in mid-January but when the early Christians fixed their own festival of the Holy Birth at the end of December, Jól was made a month earlier and incorporated into the other.

The spring festival marked the end of planting, the completion of the repairs made necessary by the wild winter weather and the beginning of the viking season. It was a time for brief relaxation and for farewells. Less religious and more romantic than Jól, it had a number of charming customs attached to it. In one of these, young girls placed a spray of spring flowers beneath their pillows so that they would dream of their future husbands. Each village also put up a large pole, or ship's mast, decorated with garlands and wreaths like the maypole of England and which became the centre of dancing, games and gossip.

A national festival took place every nine years. During the time it was celebrated, peace was proclaimed throughout the whole region. The greatest temple of Viking times was Uppsala, Sweden, and during this festival thousands of people attended from all over the country. Animals were slaughtered before images of the gods and their blood sprinkled over the altar and the worshippers. Sacrificial

A joyful maypole dance to welcome the spring

sacred grove nearby. It is recorded that during one national festival held at Leire, Denmark, ninety-nine men— criminals and slaves—as well as horses, dogs and cocks were sacrificed.

Great banquets were also held in the temples, memorial toasts being drunk to Odin and the other gods, whilst the cup of memory was raised to "the dear departed".

When Christianity became general, these toasts continued, but the worshippers now drank to Christ, Mary and the Northern Saints.

animals included sheep, goats, cattle, horses and swine, and on some occasions even men. At Uppsala, men, horses and dogs were sacrificed and their bodies hung on the branches of trees in a

The Art of the Skalds

The great hall was packed with people, eating, drinking, laughing, boasting, the warm air heavy with the scent of roast meats and of honey-mead. Then a skilled hand ran along the strings of a harp and almost immediately there came a stillness. This was the time that the company enjoyed most, the time when the skald told of the struggles and triumphs of the gods, of the great heroes of olden days, and of the brave deeds of the lord's ancestors and his own bravery in battle.

The skald was the professional minstrel of the Viking Age. The royal court had several, and there was always one at least to be found in a nobleman's house. He would stay for a while and then move on whilst another took his place. During the 9th and 10th centuries most of the skalds came from Norway, but from about 1000 they seemed to be almost wholly Icelanders, a skaldic closed shop!

Their poems were composed in special metres and many of the words and expressions they used were deliberately obscure, forcing the audience to listen most carefully in order to follow what the skald was talking about, for he seemed to take a delight in taking a familiar noun and describing it in unusual language. This playing with, and on, words was known as the "kenning".

When referring to the sea, for example, the skalds spoke of the "Whale's Road", "Land of Ran", or "Ran's Road", Ran being the goddess of the sea in its more violent moods. When calm it was "Ægir's Road", Ægir being Ran's husband. This form of verse-speaking could produce some delightful imagery. The children of Ægir and Ran were the waves—white hooded girls with shining locks. To be drowned at sea was to "go to Ran", to be dragged down in her net; she also lured ships into Ægir's open jaws. The drowned were taken to her domain; yet even this became pleasant, for the Vikings, dripping with salt water and festooned with seaweed, would be welcomed by their own kinsmen and invited to drink their own burial-ale.

The kenning made ordinary things appear much more vivid. One name used for ships, for instance, was "beasts of the sea that have lain in the boathouse until spring with heads bent low".

In early Viking times the skalds spoke (they never sang) of the great gods: of Odin, the chief of all gods, guarded by wolves and attended by ravens who brought him news from all over the world, of Thor, Frey, Loki and the rest; of Asgard, the shining home of the gods, and of Valhalla, the Hall of the Chosen. Later, when Harald Fairhair had united Norway, his campaigns and those of other mortal heroes took their place.

There were also comical poems and poems of everyday life, all made colourful and exciting by the art and genius of the skald.

The mysteries of the sea—the Goddess Ran, sea-monsters and serpents—were popular skaldic subjects. Here, Ran drags to her watery palace the warships of dead Viking heroes

Ordeal by fire: if the hot iron landed safely in the water trough, the man was halfway to being judged innocent

Laws of the Viking Age

In Viking times, free men, entitled to bear arms, gathered at special places to dispense justice and make decisions. Such an assembly was called the Thing. The most important of these was the National Thing, often presided over by the King himself, where matters of national importance were discussed. The meeting often lasted for more than a week. Those attending would reside or camp in the neighbourhood and, when not in conclave, would trade, gossip and play games and sports.

There were also Local Things, always held at a regular place, where a rock or mound would serve as a platform for the speakers. The 'thingstead' was considered sacred and was enclosed within holy ropes. Local Things were mainly held to enable one man to bring a suit against another. Thirty-six judges were elected to represent the people and the laws they upheld were clear and precise as to the way the trial should be conducted and the penalties that might be awarded. The Scandinavian word for these laws was *by-lor* from which comes "By-Law".

Sometimes, when no decision was reached, the accused had to undergo an ordeal by fire, and the judgment was left to the gods. In one of these ordeals he had to pick up a hot iron in his bare hands and carry it for nine paces. In another, he was forced to stand some distance from a trough into which he had to cast the hot iron. If it missed he had to go forward, pick it up and throw again. When either test had been completed, a mitten was placed over the burned hand and fixed with a seal. After three days the hand was inspected and the accused was judged guilty or not by its condition.

Sometimes the judges decreed that the two men in dispute should settle the argument by a duel. In one, they chose their own weapons and fought to the death. These, however, were rare. More common was a duel fought on a cloak within a marked square. The fight began on the cloak and neither man was allowed to step outside the square. It ended when blood from one or other of the contestants fell on to the cloak.

A man found guilty of murder was beheaded or hanged; stoning or drowning were the penalties for witchcraft. Frequently a man was outlawed, which meant banishment from the district or from the country for a stated number of years, or even for life. After the sentence had been passed, the outlaw was allowed time to settle his affairs and prepare for his journey. During this period no one could harm him.

A man sentenced to full outlawry was stripped of his property and no one was supposed to give him food, shelter or aid. Anyone could, if he wished, kill him without punishment. He therefore had no option other than begin a new life in another country or live with other outlaws as a robber and bandit.

In formal duels, swordblades were rarely brought into direct contact with one another; that would have spoiled their very fine edge. Instead, the blow was taken by the flat of the shield. As a result, it very quickly became battered and hacked about, and it was not unusual for each contestant to keep one or two fresh shields in reserve

THE INCREDIBLE VIKING SHIPS

"NOBODY BELIEVED that such a voyage was possible" wrote the Anglo-Saxon Alcuin when he heard about the first Viking raid on Lindisfarne. This was because no other nation was able to build such ships, nor had the courage to venture on to the high seas. Seafaring, until the time of the Vikings, was confined to short voyages in which the ships hugged the shore and would rarely venture out in anything but a flat calm. Indeed, it was not until the late Middle Ages that any other nation was able to build such strong, sea-going vessels, yet Vikings were thrusting through the North Sea with their unique ships long before 800 and, soon after this date, the Norwegians were even venturing out into the wide, stormy seas of the North Atlantic.

The secret strength of the Viking ships lay in their solid keels and in the thin clinker-built planks to which the timbers were fixed. They did not butt their way through the waves, but slid smoothly over them like a sea-bird. The ships had a shallow draught, and this was to prove invaluable for it enabled them to creep stealthily along night-darkened rivers and, at morning light, strike terror into the surrounding countryside. They had one mast carrying a single large sail, striped or chequered. The ships were very fast and remained buoyant in seas that would have destroyed other types of vessels. They were also easy to handle and the Viking could beach them on an enemy shore and run them off again with a speed that often made all the difference between failure and success on some of their "strike and run" raids.

The size of a Viking ship was known by the number of oars it carried. One with sixteen rowing benches was called a "sixteen-seater" and so on. The most common of all Viking longships was that with twenty pairs of oars, carrying forty oarsmen and usually another sixty or so men. The famous "dragon ships" were in the great ship class, which had twenty-five or more pairs of oars. They got their name from the curved and gilded dragon's head that rose at the prow.

Another type of ship were the *knörrs*. These were wider and higher than the fighting ships and were built to carry cargo and supplies and also to transport

Cross-section of a "knörr" ship for transporting Scandinavian settlers, their goods and live-stock to Iceland

Long-buried ships reconstructed and preserved in the Viking Ship Hall, Oslo. Above: the Oseberg, light, low-sided, a luxury vessel for cruising in shallow waters. Below: the Gokstad, more heavily built, a true ocean-going craft. In 1893 a replica of the Gokstad ship was successfully navigated across the Atlantic from Bergen to Newfoundland

troops. They were also used for long voyages in stormy seas: Bjarni's ship, used later by Leif and Thorvald, was a *knörr*. This type had fewer rowing benches than a longship and relied almost entirely on its sailing powers. Its hull was one large hold and anything stored in this was protected against waves and rain by a large sail stretched across it.

More is known about the Viking ships than any other period until those of comparatively recent times. This is because three, the Oseberg, the Gokstad and the Tune ships, named after the places where they were found, were discovered in graves and are remarkably well preserved. They are now in the Viking Ship Hall at Bygday, Oslo. Another five Viking ships, two merchantmen, two warships and a lighter craft—probably a fishing boat—have recently been salvaged from the bed of the Roskilde Fjord, in Denmark. They had been sunk on purpose nine hundred years ago to prevent enemy fleets from sailing up the fjord to the wealthy trading centre of Roskilde. The larger merchant ship is noteworthy as being the only existing example of a *knorr*, the Viking deep sea trader described already in this chapter; and the larger of the two warships is 28 metres long, the longest Viking ship ever recovered. The lighter fishing craft is remarkable for the boatbuilder's axemarks which can still be seen clearly on its timbers.

All these ships are evidence of the bold seamanship and fine craftsmanship of the days when the Scandinavian peoples were the undisputed masters of the seas, and without them our know-ledge of Viking culture would be far poorer.

Oseberg—A Queen's Grave

A large tumulus, or mound of earth and stones, had kept a quiet vigil on a plain near the Oseberg Farm in Norway for a thousand years. Then, in 1903, a party of archaeologists began to dig into it. They made a fabulous discovery. There, surprisingly well preserved, lay the remains of a magnificent Viking ship built at the beginning of the 9th century, 21·5 metres long and 5·1 metres wide at its widest part.

It is clear, however, that the Oseberg ship, as it is now called, was not designed for fighting men to go a-viking in, or for long voyages on the high seas. It is built light and low, equipped for both sail and oars, but suitable only for gentle cruising in fair weather and over calm waters. The elegantly arched prow, tapering into a slender spiral, would never have withstood the buffeting of the North Sea, for example.

The Oseberg ship is most famous as a beautiful example of the fine wood craftsmanship of the Viking Era: along the ship's gunwales and between the waterline and the prow and stern are carved intricate intertwining animal patterns, and the fifteen pairs of pine oars, all found intact, are beautifully wrought, each finishing in a graceful curve. A strip of pine ran around the ship's oaken sides so that shields could be hung along it when sailing in calm weather. It must have made a magnificent sight, gliding nobly between local

62

Reconstruction of a tapestry found on the Oseberg ship, showing spear-carrying warriors in procession

ports along the Norwegian coastline.

The archæologists found far more than just the ship. At its after-part they discovered a large, wooden burial chamber in which were the remains of two women, one old, the other young. It is believed that they were Queen Asa, grandmother of King Harald Fairhair, and her serving woman. The ship which had probably served the young queen as a luxury cruising vessel in life had thus become her elaborate coffin. The chamber was fully furnished with beds, quilts, pillows and blankets and three studded oak chests. One of the chests was almost entirely preserved and its lid swung easily back on its hinges, even after having lain buried for more than a thousand years. Within were a collection of personal domestic items—a wool-holder, a comb, a pair of scissors and so on—all necessary for a lady setting out on a long journey.

Nearby were three richly carved wooden sleighs and a heavy oaken cart inworked with scenes of human figures. On the long side of the cart, in the centre of a strange flock of wild animals, is shown a small procession. A man with a raised sword holds his enemy's horse by the bridle, but is hindered in his assault on the unarmed horseman by a woman who holds his sword hand by the wrist.

Other objects found in the tomb included some strange barrels, kitchen equipment, plates, jugs, iron cauldrons and a hand-mill.

No remains of royal residences of the Viking Era have been found in Norway, but a glimpse of their typical contents has been provided by the considerable findings at the Oseberg burial ship, particularly the kind of personal possessions and domestic utensils surrounding a high-born lady.

ARMS
AND
ARMOUR

THE SKALDS, or minstrels, of Viking times, never, to use a modern expression, liked "to call a spade a spade". Instead they would give strange yet beautifully poetic names for many proper nouns. For example the sword, the noble weapon beloved of Viking king and chieftain, was called the 'Fire of Battle'. 'Lightning Flash of Blood' and 'The Battle-storm's Fish'. Some warriors gave their swords a personal name such as 'Keen', 'Fierce', 'Long-and-sharp', 'Gold-hilt' and so on. These names reveal the importance that they placed on their swords, many of which were handed down from father to son.

The Viking sword was of iron, long, broad and double-edged, about 90cms. long. There was a short, straight guard at the broad end of the blade, a grip, and then another cross-piece surmounted by a triangular or semi-circular pommel. Although most of the more common Viking swords were made within Scandinavia, the blades of the finer weapons were usually forged in France, or Germany. The hilts and pommels, however, were usually made by Scan-

dinavian craftsmen using ivory, gold and silver; some were truly magnificent.

The blades that were imported into Scandinavia were tough, light and well balanced. This was an important factor, for sword fighting was then a matter of sweeping strokes in which the edge rather than the point of the weapon was used. Many of those found bear the maker's name. One such name is "Ulfberth". This firm began making blades in Germany about 900 and exported them into Scandinavia through Hedeby.

Above: a Viking's head carved from elk-horn illustrates the typical cone-shaped helmet with noseguard. Right: a Scandinavian chieftain, wearing the visored helmet reserved for high-ranking warriors, instructs his men to take up battle position on a hilltop

64

The other most important sword-smiths marked their blades "Ingelri". These were made by the Franks.

The swords were placed in a wooden scabbard, usually covered with tooled leather, and at first hung from a baldric on the left side of the body. Later it hung from a sword-hilt buckled around the Viking's waist.

There were many references to swords in the sagas, and some are given magical properties, especially those which were said to be made by the dwarfs in forges hidden away deep in mountain caves. The great hero Sigurd had such a sword. When it was newly forged, he raised it high above his head and brought it down on the anvil. The sword remained bright and unmarked, yet the anvil lay at his feet in two pieces. He then went down to the river and held his sword in the water. So very fine was the blade that a single strand of wool, allowed to float down with the current on to the sword's edge, was sheared clean in two.

Another famous sword belonged to King Hakon. It was called 'Quern-biter' for, to test its strength, he struck a quern—a heavy stone used for grinding corn—and split it in two.

The other main weapon of the Viking was, of course, his battle-axe. There were two types. One was the 'bearded axe', a favourite weapon in sea fights where it was used for grappling and boarding. The other was the dreaded broad-axe: its blade was sometimes as broad as one foot, and it was so heavy that it could be used only when gripped with both hands. It was the broad-axe, rather than the sword, which was to become the symbol of the Viking raiders.

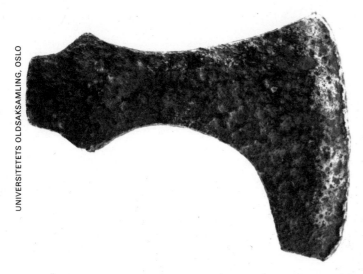

UNIVERSITETETS OLDSAKSAMLING, OSLO

The iron head of a typical broad-axe, found in Norway

The Viking's third weapon was the spear. Like the axe, it was of two main types. One was the javelin, with a thin and light blade for throwing; the other was the lance, fitted with a broad and heavy blade for fighting at close quarters.

The sagas often refer to skill in spear casting, especially that of catching a javelin thrown by the enemy, swinging the arm about and returning it, blade foremost, at the enemy!

Olav Tryggvason, the Norse Viking king, was able to throw two javelins at once, using both hands.

Bows and arrows are also mentioned in the sagas and were important weapons in Viking battles, the "arrow-fall" constantly being compared to heavy rain. No bows or arrow shafts have been discovered, but arrow-heads are frequently found in graves, often in bundles.

The other weapon was the iron knife, tool as well as weapon, which was carried in the belt by men and, frequently, suspended on a chain around the neck of women. This was known as a *sax*.

The Viking shield was round and wooden. It was strengthened by iron bars at the back, some of which served as a grip. A round iron boss was placed in the centre and the shield itself was sometimes painted or left in its natural wood colour. These were the shields that were hung along the sides of the gunwales of Viking ships in calm seas, or when rowed along the smooth water of a fjord. They were usually about a metre in diameter.

The warrior wore a small conical helmet. Later, nose guards were added of the type made familiar in the Bayeux tapestry. None has been found which has the great bull or ox horns projecting from its sides—the type of helmet commonly associated with the fierce Vikings—but carvings showing warriors wearing such helmets have been discovered.

Kings and nobles wore shirts made of interlinked iron rings. The rest wore jerkins of leather with iron or bone plaques sewn on to them for extra protection. In the chronicle of the Irish wars, the *Codagh,* the writer states that the Vikings were triumphant "because of the excellence of their polished, ample, treble, heavy, trusty, glittering corslets, and their hard, strong, valiant swords; and their well-riveted long spears".

The Viking kings had an elite corps of fighters who scorned mail-coats and even jerkins. When they went into battle they fought bare-chested and a kind of madness overcame them so that they became more like frenzied beasts than human beings. From their strange behaviour comes the phrase—*berserk*—the fury of battle. There is even a suggestion that the uncanny Werewolf superstition was involved, for others, very similar, were called wolf-skins, and many believed that these men could turn themselves into bears and wolves and fight with all the ferocity of those animals.

Although it is the sea and ships which instantly come to mind when thinking of Vikings, yet they rode a great deal on horseback. At the moment of actual battle, however, they always dismounted to fight on foot. Their horses were splendidly equipped, the saddles, bridles and other harness being decorated and ornamented. In one grave, for example, some spurs and stirrups beautifully inlaid with silver have been discovered, proving that the Viking's horse was as well turned out as himself.

An elaborate sword hilt found in a Viking burial ground in the Western Isles of Scotland

Fighting on Land and Sea

It is easy to understand why the Vikings were feared by the people of the countries they attacked. Everything was in their favour. They would arrive, as if from nowhere, at a monastery or settlement and use their speed and mobility, the element of surprise and the terror that their reputation inspired to attack, kill, loot and then disappear like will-o'-the-wisps.

By the time the local English chieftain had gathered his men together and had brought them, panting with the exertion, to the scene, the Vikings had long gone, their ships heavy with loot and slaves. It was only later, when they came to settle in a country and thus enable the army of that country time to assemble, or when they were met at sea by equal fleets, as during the reign of Alfred, that the Viking was called upon to fight for his life.

They knew little of strategy, for they relied mainly upon the skill and bravery of their individual warriors. Their naval actions were particularly unimaginative, for no manoeuvring was permitted. They would rope and chain their ships together, lower the masts and then, like a floating fortress, row them into action. No ship could fight as a single unit unless it cut itself loose from the rest, and this was only done to escape destruction.

The opposing fleets would fire at each other with stones and arrows and then, when their bows were touching, the fighting would become hand-to-hand between the men crowding on to the fore parts of the opposing ships. This was the post of honour and was given to the best warriors. Whenever possible the men of the Viking Age preferred to fight in the shelter of a fjord or river where smooth water made boarding less hazardous.

Land battles also showed little imagination. The opposing forces were generally drawn up in four divisions—centre, two wings and the reserve. After the usual exchange of arrows, javelins and stones, the armies marched forward but, once they met, there was no overall control. The battle became little more than hundreds, or thousands of men fighting in single combat and, until a leader was killed or men began to run away, there was little way of knowing how the battle was going. The opposing chieftains were always in the centre with their personal bodyguards and their standard-bearers responsible for the battle banner. Some of these banners became famous, some were even believed to have magic powers. Harald Hardrada's was called "The Land-waster"; King Sverri of Norway had "The Victory-fly" and there were many more, with similar stirring names.

If the chief and his banner were threatened, his bodyguard would form a protective "wall" in which every shield touched his neighbour's and would hold firm until victory or death.

Sometimes the armies attacked in a wedge-shaped formation called "swine-order" in which the picked men of the van formed the "swine-snout". This was supposed to break the enemy's line and thrust deep into his ranks but it also had a disadvantage—the end of the "snout" might be cut off by opposing warriors closing in from either side.

After battle the slain would be buried and the wounded taken away for treatment. The booty, armour and weapons of the defeated were collected and shared and then, no doubt, the victors were glad to rest.

A skirmish at sea between rival Viking fleets. The ships on the left have earned themselves a temporary advantage by getting into good battle order early, while some of those on the right are still lowering their sails and lashing themselves together

OF GODS AND HEROES

ICELAND WAS settled by a number of petty kings and chieftains from Western Norway who refused to live under Harald Fairhair, preferring to seek a new life with their families on the recently discovered island. Each king or chieftain took a large area of land and there he ruled his people as he had done in Norway. In time these separate families prospered and multiplied.

Although Norwegians formed the main part of the new Icelandic community, there were also settlers from Sweden, Denmark and even Celts, all seeking breathing space and a new life.

The Icelanders' public affairs were well-ordered, their laws being dispensed at the *Althing*, the all-island parliament. Their domestic life was simple, and although it was a harder existence than that of their former homeland, they were content enough.

During the long dark nights of winter while they sat by their fires and while the men made nets or polished their weapons and the women wove or spun, one of their number would retell the old stories of the gods, kings and heroes of the 'old country'. The children listened and learned the stories by heart, and in time, passed them on to their children.

For generations, none of these stories was written down because few people knew how to write. At last, round about 1125, Ari Frodi wrote down in the old Norse tongue "histories relating to times ancient and modern". He collected many of the tales brought to Iceland by the early settlers, and put them into one volume. (The name 'saga' comes from the Icelandic *Segin Saga* meaning 'a tale told'). He called it the *Islendingabok,* the history of Iceland from the time of the early settlers until the year 1120.

Ari also collected the history of the lives of all the kings of Norway and the pedigree of the Icelandic settlers, valuable information which went into a saga, the *Landnamabok,* which was continually being added to by others until 1220.

A number of romantic, rather than historical, sagas were also written. One of these is the *Saga of Burnt Njal,* by an unknown author. It is placed at the end of the 10th century and has Njal, the mythical Lawman of Judgement and Peace as its hero.

Another is the *Grettissaga*, or Saga of Gretti the Strong, who was a famous outlaw. This saga contains a great deal of incidental information about myths and superstitions of the time.

One of the greatest of all saga writers was Snorri Sterluson, author of the *Heimskringla*, or "Sagas of the Norwegian Kings", and of others which retell the myths and superstitions of his pagan ancestry.

Sagas are always written in a straightforward manner as if meant to be read aloud to a group of interested listeners. Sentences generally are short, simple and full of interest and packed with details of the costume, armour and weapons of the main characters. Dialogue is rarely used, the saga writers preferring to concentrate on the heroic actions of their heroes.

Taken together, the sagas tell of the creation of the world, the wonders and mysteries of nature, the stories of gods and goddesses, the strange world of giants and dwarfs, trolls and elves, and, of course, of kings, chieftains and heroes, both real and imaginary. From such sagas much is learned of the generosity, heroism and camaraderie of the Vikings.

A skald holds his audience spellbound with tales of long-dead heroes. His favourite themes were valour, loyalty and honesty

Above: Odin sits enthroned at Gladsheim, listening intently to what his ravens have to tell of man's misdeeds on Earth. Below, right: silver and bronze figurines representing the Valkyries

The Great Gods

The great gods of the Vikings lived in Asgard which was connected to the Earth by a colourful bridge called Bifröst, but which men call the rainbow. The bridge was guarded by Heimdall, the watchman of the gods, whose hearing was said to be so keen that he could hear wool growing on the back of a sheep and grass growing in a field.

The greatest of the gods was Odin, the creator of Man and the maker of Heaven and Earth. He lived with the other gods in a vast mansion called Gladsheim where, in the great hall called Valhalla, he sat on his throne Hlidskjalk and watched what was going on in the world. His two ravens—Hugin and Mumin—flew out each morning and on their return at night would perch on his shoulders to tell him of man's doings. He was also attended by Valkyries, thirteen beautiful warrior-maidens, who watched the course of battles and chose those heroes who fell in the fighting whom they considered worthy of reward.

Fully armed with shield, helmet and spear, and mounted on fierce warhorses which bore them across the sky, they carried the heroes across the rainbow bridge to Valhalla. Here, in the Great Hall, the heroes feasted with Odin and fought over and over again the battles in which they had won undying fame.

Odin had seven sons. They were Thor, twins Hödur and Balder, Vithar the silent god, Bragi the god of wisdom and poetry, Ali, and Tyr.

Frey was the god of the harvest, of sunshine and of rain. He was also the god of seafarers and his own ship, *Skidbladnir*, was large enough to carry all the gods yet could be folded up and put into his pocket. His sister was Freya, the goddess of love and healing, of marriage and birth. She rode in a chariot drawn by white cats, emblems of fertility.

Loki was the god of evil, of passion and jealousy, and was himself respons-ible for many murders and a great deal of mischief. His three children by the giantess Angurboda were as hateful as himself. They were Fenri, a hideous and massive wolf which finally had to be bound by a magic chain forged by the dwarfs; an even more dreadful creature called the Serpent of Midgard, and Hel, goddess of the dead.

There were also other gods and goddesses including the strange Norns, the three goddesses of fate. Their names were Urda, Verdardi and Skuld, representing the past, present and future.

The Vikings believed that the whole Earth was surrounded by a vast ocean, home of the Midgard Serpent. On its far shore lay huge mountains, where the giants lived in their citadel of Utgard. Beneath the Earth lay the domain of Hel, the land of the dead.

Although the names of most of these Viking gods have long been forgotten,

73

Carved on an ancient Swedish picture-stone, a Viking warrior rides into Valhalla on an eight-legged horse. One of Odin's Valkyrie maidens holds up a drinking horn in welcome

four are in common use wherever the English language is spoken, for from them come the names of four of the seven days of the week.

From Tyr (*Tiw* in Anglo-Saxon) comes *Tiwes Daeg*, or TUESDAY.

From Odin (*Woden* in Anglo-Saxon) comes Woden's Day, or WEDNESDAY.

From Thor comes Thor's Day, or THURSDAY.

Lastly, from Freya comes Freya's Day, or FRIDAY.

Thor and his Hammer

Odin may have been the chief of the Nordic gods, but Thor was the most popular—for he was the god of the people. Red-bearded, strong, and friendly except when roused, he was continually setting off with his mighty hammer, Mjollnir, to do battle with his sworn enemies, the giants. He would travel in a carriage drawn by two he-goats and, when he sped through the clouds, thunder crashed down and rumbled behind him.

To the peasant he was very real, a god who would go out of his way to help humans. He made crops grow by sending the rain, he was called upon to bless marriages, he sent the sailor favourable winds, and warriors prayed to him for victory. He was a hard-working, all-round god.

Clasped about his waist he had a Belt of Strength to give him strength beyond all others, and he had a special pair of iron gloves that he had to wear before he could wield Mjollnir. This hammer never failed him. When he hurled it through the air it always found its mark and then would return to his hand. Very often the stroke was preceded by thunder and lightning.

It was a Norse custom, when a child was born, for it to be signed by Thor's hammer to show it had become part of the family, and also for men to call upon Thor to hallow their marriage ceremonies with Mjollnir. Hammer amulets were worn to guard against misfortune.

There was one terrible morning when, on waking, Thor felt at his side and found that the precious hammer had gone. He called Loki, the craftiest of the gods, to help him. Loki duly visited the land of the giants, but returned with grave news. Thrym, lord of all the giants, had stolen the hammer and had buried it eight miles beneath the earth. It would only be returned if Freya, the beautiful goddess of love and fertility, agreed to become his wife. She naturally refused to agree to this suggestion and Loki came forward with a clever scheme.

Thor was dressed as a bride, with a veil about his face, and household keys jangling at his waist. Loki was disguised as his serving maid, and together they journeyed to Thrym's court. The lord of the giants believed Thor to be Freya, and although at times, whilst

On the lower half of this picture stone from Uppland, Sweden, Thor the God of Thunder sits in a ship, holding his hammer Mjollnir in his right hand and fishing for the monster World Serpent with his left

Thor and his hammer were inseparable. The sculptor of this Icelandic bronze statuette dating from about 1000 A.D. has represented him clutching it with both hands. The hammer symbol was carried by the religious in the form of an amulet, and played an important part in family ceremony: it was used to bless brides and the newly-born, and to consecrate burials

they were dining, he became suspicious, Loki always had a ready answer. When he commented on the amount of food that 'Freya' was consuming Loki said, "She has fasted for eight nights, she was so eager to come to you," and when he remarked that her eyes were bright and terrible Loki replied, "She has had no sleep for eight nights, she was so eager to come to this marriage feast".

Finally Thrym said, "Bring in the hammer of Thor to hallow the bride. Lay it on the maiden's knee."

This done, Thor threw the bridal veil aside, leapt to his feet and, snatching up his hammer, struck out all round him, killing Thrym and many of his giant warriors. Thus avenged, he and Loki returned to Asgard where the other gods rejoiced to see that he had successfully regained the mighty Mjollnir.

Balder the Fair

Odin, the All-Father, had received a terrible warning from a prophetess. His second son, Balder the Fair and the Good, was fated to die. His death, ironically, was to be brought about by Balder's own twin brother, Hödur, the blind god of darkness. This was terrible news indeed, for, with the one exception of Loki, the evil one, Balder was beloved by all.

Hoping to avert the doom, the gods sat in high council and it was finally decided to exact an oath from all things—beasts, birds and reptiles, iron and other metals, fire and water, everything in fact that could injure or kill—that not one of them would harm

Balder, unaware of his terrible fate, smiles as Hödur prepares with Loki's help to throw the deadly mistletoe dart

Balder. All swore this oath for they all loved him.

When this great oath had been given and received, the gods soon found Balder's invincibility a source of amusement and sport. He would stand against a mark at their meetings and smile as some hurled stones and spears or others struck at him with their swords and battle-axes. None of these weapons harmed him or gave him the slightest concern, for the iron and the stones remembered their solemn oath. But Loki, jealous of Balder and of the love that all had for him, longed to bring him down. He took on the shape of an old woman and went to Frigga, the great goddess to whom the oath had been given. He remarked that he had seen the gods assaulting Balder, yet he received no hurt. He then asked, "Is there *nothing* that can harm him?"

Frigga answered, "There is but one thing. There is a little shrub called mistletoe which I thought too young and too feeble to ask to swear the oath like the rest."

Soon afterwards Loki, having made himself invisible, arrived at the place where the gods were amusing themselves. Moving closer to Hödur he asked him why he did not join in the sport. The other answered that he did not know where Balder was standing, that he had nothing to throw and in any case he was blind. Then Loki put a sharpened dart of mistletoe in Hödur's hand and, guiding his arm, sped the dart towards the young god. Balder fell dead instantly.

After a brief period of mourning, Hermod, Balder's brother, said that he would ride to Hel, the goddess of the dead, and beg her to allow Balder to return to the land of the living.

Whilst he was on his journey, Balder's body was laid in his great ship *Ring-horn* and a funeral pyre was laid about it. At this sight, Balder's wife Nanna gave a great cry and fell dead also, of a broken heart. Her body was laid by the side of her husband's, the pyre was lit and the great ship drifted out to sea.

When Hermod reached Hel he was promised that if all things on earth wept for Balder he would return again to Asgard. Overjoyed, for he knew all things loved his son, Odin sent messengers to every part of the land where everyone, and everything, duly wept at Balder's death. As the messengers were returning to Asgard, they found

The body of a Viking hero sets out on its last voyage, as Balder did on "Ring-horn", while his companions shoot flaming arrows on to the deck to turn the ship into a floating funeral pyre. A scene from the film "The Vikings" (United Artists)

an old hag crouched in a cave, but she only said, "Let Hel keep what is hers. I will only weep dry tears for Balder. What is he to me?" and the messengers sadly went on their way, not realising that the "hag" was Loki in disguise.

So Balder never returned, but the sagas foretold that one day he would come back to a new, beautiful and verdant earth and live once again with those he had known and loved.

Loki's Punishment

For many years, the gods and goddesses in Asgard had been abused and slighted by Loki. He loved evil for its own sake and enjoyed being evil himself, taking a delight in seeing how bad he could be without being punished for his ill-doing. By his part in the death of Balder, however, he finally went too far. Odin was determined to punish him for this great crime and Loki, as if suddenly realising what he had done, fled from Asgard to the mountains. Here he built himself a strange house which had four doors, opening to the north, south, east and west, allowing him to keep a watch on all sides.

Yet even in his remote mountain hide-away he could not avoid the all-seeing eye of Odin who looked out over the world and saw Loki seated before his hiding place, busily making a net from flax and yarn. Odin called some of the gods to him and ordered them to hurry and capture Loki before he could escape, but the other saw them coming and, throwing his half-completed net into a fire, changed himself into a salmon and plunged into a nearby river.

When the gods arrived at his home they found it empty. One of their number, however, saw the net smouldering in the fire and pulled it out. After they had examined it they decided to make another like it—for this was the first net that had ever been made.

When the net was completed, Thor took one end, the rest of the gods took hold of the other and they threw it into the river. At first Loki escaped by hiding between two stones, but when they weighted it and dragged it along the river bed, they saw a great salmon leap out of the water in an attempt to escape. Thor threw himself into the river and grasped the fish. It flapped and jerked violently in an effort to escape from his grasp. But Thor held it fast by the tail and brought it ashore. This is said to be the reason why the tail of a salmon is fine and thin.

Loki was forced to return to his usual form and brought to trial. His sentence was a terrible one. He was taken to a cavern and bound to three vicious sharp-edged rocks. To add to his suffering, the goddess Skadi placed a serpent above him so that, drop by drop, its poison would fall on his face. Only one person had any pity for Loki. That was his wife, Siguna, who constantly stood by his side, cup in hand, catching the drops of venom as they fell, turning aside to empty it when it became full.

During those moments a few drops fell on him causing him to scream with agony and struggle so violently in his bands that the earth shook and trembled. And that, to the Vikings of old, was the cause of what men call earthquakes.

Loki's punishment: his violent struggles were believed to be the cause of earthquakes

"Hairy Breeches" and his Sons

A famous Viking and hero of a great many sagas was a Dane, Ragnar Lodbrok. When a young man he fell in love with Thora, a beautiful princess who lived in a castle surrounded by a moat in which lived hundreds of large and poisonous snakes. Ragnar was determined to win her so he dressed himself in animal skins, hairy side outwards, and coated them with pitch as protec-

tion against the serpent's fangs. He crossed the moat safely, won the princess, and gained himself a new name—*Lodbrok*, or 'Hairy Breeches'.

He spent a great deal of his life a-viking and became famous when in 845, with a fleet of 120 ships, he sailed up the Seine to attack Paris. Charles the Bald, King of the West Franks, seeing the threat to his capital, halved his army, spreading his men out along either bank, ready to resist the Vikings on whatever bank they landed. This was a fatal move: Ragnar's entire army leapt ashore on one bank and, whilst the Franks opposite watched in horror, hanged more than a hundred of the defeated enemy as a sacrifice to Odin.

Ragnar's army entered Paris on Easter Sunday and, after plundering it, prepared to return home, his ships heavy with captives and loot. Charles now had a great opportunity to block the river and prevent the ship's return, especially as many of the Vikings were ill from fever brought on by a dense and clinging mist. Instead he paid Ragnar 7,000 pounds of silver—the first ever 'Danegeld'—and was relieved to see the dragon heads of the longships heading down river towards the sea.

Ragnar's death was a strange one. He was harrying in England when he was surprised and taken prisoner by Ella, King of Northumbria. He was thrown into a pit full of snakes at York but this time he did not have the protection of his 'hairy breeches'. Before he died, or so the saga says, he thought of his sons and remarked, grimly, "The piglings would be grunting if they knew the plight of the boar!"

His words were prophetic. Three of his sons, Ivar the Boneless, Ubbi and Halfdan came raging across the North Sea to avenge his death. They fought and killed Ella, went on to conquer York, London and all East Anglia and finally founded what are still known as the Five Boroughs: Lincoln, Stamford, Leicester, Derby and Nottingham.

Another son, Björn Ironside, undertook the longest of all Viking raids: during his epic voyage he fought the Moors in the Mediterranean, plundered the Rhone Valley and harried Northern Italy. It is told that he and his fellow Vikings returned with a number of black prisoners. As Björn sailed to Ireland after this voyage, they must have caused something of a sensation!

Ragnar in the snake-pit

The Saga of Olaf Tryggvason

One of the greatest of all Vikings was Olaf, son of Tryggi Olafsson and a great-grandson of Norway's first king, Harald Fairhair. Even as a child his life was marked by danger and adventure. His mother, Queen Astrid, was forced to flee from Norway to Russia where her brother, Sigurd, had a high position at the court of Valdmir the king. On the way, however, their ship was captured by Vikings and the boy and his mother were separated and sold into slavery.

Some years later Sigurd happened to see Olaf and, greatly taken by the lad, made enquiries about him. He soon realised that the other was his nephew and, after buying his freedom, took him back to Russia.

When he reached his 'teens, Olaf became a Viking. He haunted the Baltic, harried Gotland and fought a battle in Denmark. He later turned his ship's prows to ravage in Germany, in the Low Countries and finally the British Isles. In 994 he helped Sven Forkbeard to attack London and, although his fellow Vikings were driven off, Olaf continued to plunder the countryside until bought off by King Aethelred. He also became a Christian at this time and swore never to return to England except in peace.

By now he had been away from the land of his birth for many years and a longing came over him to return to Norway, although Earl Hakon now ruled as overlord of the country. Olaf set sail with five ships, taking a number of Christian priests with him.

When near the Norwegian coast he sighted three ships commanded by Erland, Hakon's son, and after a brief fight Erland was killed. When the news of this reached Hakon, he feared for his life. He went into hiding but was

Queen Astrid and young Olaf are sold into slavery

murdered by his own thrall. Olaf then ascended the throne to great acclaim.

His reign was a strange one. He was determined to spread Christianity throughout the country by any means, and many who refused baptism were executed or driven into exile. He moved about the country like a fierce storm wind, smashing idols and erecting churches in their place. He particularly detested magicians and, learning that the market town of Tunsberg harboured a great many, he invited them to a great banquet and plied them with wine. When most of them were snoring in drunken slumber he set fire to the hall. Only one escaped.

In the year 1000 he was returning to Norway with a fleet of sixty ships including his own *Long Serpent*, the largest and finest Viking ship afloat. Most of his ships had gone on ahead and he was sailing in company with only eleven others when he was attacked by a combined fleet commanded by the kings of Denmark and Sweden and Eric, the exiled son of Earl Hakon.

Although greatly outnumbered, Olaf fought a battle which is considered the most heroic in Viking history. At the end of a long struggle both the Danish and Swedish kings had been forced to retire. Only Eric was left. He ran his ship alongside Olaf's battered *Long Serpent*. His Norsemen poured on to her deck and mowed down the few survivors. Realising that the battle was lost, Olaf gave a loud cry of defiance and jumped overboard.

It was said that he was secretly rescued by another ship and went to the Holy Land to live and die as a hermit. Whatever his fate, he was never seen again in the North.

Olaf—Viking and Saint

When he was only twelve years old, Olaf Haraldsson went a-viking and by the time he was fourteen had become known as a fearless and adventurous warrior. He harried in Denmark, Sweden and Finland, then joined Thorkell the Tall in a raid upon England. When Thorkell took service with king Aethelred, Olaf took his own ship to the Continent, where he fought in France and Spain.

When he was eighteen, he and some of his followers were baptised as Christians; this was to change his life completely. In 1014 he sailed to England with the exiled King Aethelred and helped him to capture London by pulling down the bridge. He later returned to Norway, an unhappy and divided country since the death of Olaf Tryggvason. He brought only two merchant ships but was welcomed by many of the people and later, at a Great Thing, was acclaimed King of all Norway.

Spring brought Sven Forkbeard and a large fleet but, although Sven's army was larger, Olaf's men were better warriors, better equipped and with white shields on each of which was emblazoned a golden cross. It was a long, hard fought battle but Olaf gained the victory and utterly routed his enemy. Sven himself fled to Russia where he died.

Olaf was now a king indeed and few, if any, of his subjects dared to refer to him by his earlier name of Olaf the Fat! He was now King Olaf II of Norway.

He was buried near the field of battle but after a year was re-buried in Nidanos where, as Adam of Bremen said, "rests the grave of the blessed Olaf, king and martyr, at whose grave God to this day performs great wonders of healing . . .".

The story of his brave deeds were told in many lands, and churches were dedicated to St. Olaf throughout Western Europe.

He began a great campaign to make Norway a Holy Christian country and, for his success, history has deemed him 'Saint'. Like the former Olaf, however, he "converted" by sword, fire and exile. In addition, he introduced new laws and reorganised his church on the lines of the English Church, bringing in bishops and priests from England.

About 1024 Knut, already king of England and Denmark, sent his son Sveinn with a huge fleet to wrest the crown from Olaf, who was forced to retreat. It was mid-winter, and with only a small band of followers Olaf had to struggle through the thick snow of the mountain passes. But he gathered strength when joined soon after by his half-brother Harold Hardrada and his following of men. Together they finally faced the invading army at Stiklar-stadir. Olaf's small army fought against great odds, the battle beginning at midday in bright sunlight. As men fell, however, the sky became an angry red and before the battle ended it was as dark as night. The king fought bravely but at last, tired and wounded, he "was brought to bay by broad-axe and spear and died of three fearful strokes".

Olaf Haraldsson meets his death from the blow of a broad-axe

THE END OF THE VIKING AGE

later, and Harald became king of the whole country in 1047.

Nineteen years later, Earl Tostig asked for Harald's help in wresting the crown of England from his half brother, Harold Goodwinson. In Harald he found a ready ally, although the Norwegian king had no doubt whose head

ONE OF the greatest of all Norse Vikings was Harald Haraldsson who, in time, was to earn the name of Hardrada, the 'hard-ruler'. But Harald Hardrada was also destined to be the last of the invaders from Scandinavia to make a determined bid to conquer England, and the last, indeed, to threaten seriously any part of Western Europe. . . . The Viking Age was drawing to a close.

When Harald was only fifteen years old, he saw his brother, King Olaf II, killed defending his Norwegian throne. He escaped to Russia and later sailed south to become a leader of the Varangian guard in Constantinople He soon gained a number of victories for his master the Caliph and remained in his employ for eight years.

On learning, however, that his nephew, Magnus the Good, was to be king of Norway he hurried back to claim a throne that he considered to be his. Harald was now a famous general and a very rich man and Magnus, rather than fight, preferred to negotiate. So, in return for half Harald's wealth, Magnus gave Harald a part of his kingdom. Magnus died two years would finally wear the English crown ... his own!

His fleet set sail in the autumn and, when it was joined by Tostig and his reinforcements, it consisted of 300 ships carrying 9000 men. After some ravaging along the English coast, the fleet sailed up the Ouse to Riccall,

Harald Hardrada falls at the Battle of Stamford Bridge, "the last true Viking chieftain to die on foreign soil". One year later, his body was brought back to Norway and buried at Nidaros, where he had founded a church. Although Harald's few surviving followers were hounded for the twelve miles back to their ships at Riccall, Harold of England spared many of them, including Olaf, the dead king's son

where the army disembarked. Harald led it towards York, smashing through an English army led by Edwin of Mercia and Morcar of Northumbria and, when they neared York, Tostig went on ahead and persuaded the garrison to surrender. It was agreed that the Norsemen should enter the city on the following day.

Monday, September 25th, 1066 was very hot, so hot in fact that most of Harald's army did not bother to put on their mailshirts. As they neared York, however, a cloud of dust made them pause. At first Harald thought it was some local chieftains with their retainers who had come to surrender; then he saw the dragon banner of Wessex flaunting against the blue sky. Harold of England, learning of the invasion, had brought his housecarls by forced marches up from the south. Harold, himself descended from Danish Vikings through his mother, was determined to throw this Norse invader back into the sea.

The two armies met at Stamford Bridge but before the battle began English envoys told Tostig that if he would make peace Harold would make him Earl of Northumbria.

"What does my brother offer my ally, Harald of Norway?" Tostig shouted in reply.

"To Harald of Norway, Harold of England will give seven feet of English ground or as much more as he may be taller than other men," was the curt answer.

As the *Anglo-Saxon Chronicle* related, "A very stubborn battle was fought by both sides." But when an arrow struck Harald in the throat the battle was almost over—"The remaining Norwegians were put to flight, while the English fiercely assailed their rear."

With the defeat of Harald of Norway, the Viking Age was virtually at an end. The link between the Vikings and the kings of England, however, was not entirely broken. King Harold of England was himself killed not long afterwards at the Battle of Hastings by the invading William of Normandy, who then succeeded to the throne. The new king, although from north-west France, was a descendant of Vikings from Norway and Denmark who had made repeated raids on the French coast in the early tenth century.

The events leading to William's accession to the English throne began in the summer of 911, when a meeting took place between Charles the Simple, King of the West Franks, the inhabitants of what is now western France, and the Viking leader, Rollo, who had been terrorising Charles' coastal waters and river estuaries for so long.

William of Normandy, descendant of Vikings, who was to become William I of England

Charles had a proposition to make. He offered Rollo a large part of the coastal area of Western France if he agreed to do several things. He had to become a Christian; he had to swear to protect his new land from all the King's enemies; he had to marry the king's daughter. He had also to pay homage to the king, accepting him as his liege lord. Rollo agreed at first, but when he learned that the act of homage meant that he should kneel and kiss the king's foot he was furious—his Viking pride did not allow such an act.

But there was too much at stake to refuse this token gesture, so he ordered one of his men to do it for him. The other walked forward but, instead of kneeling, he seized the royal foot and brought it up to his mouth. There was a bellow of laughter from the other Vikings as the king toppled backwards and lay flat on the ground. It was a strange beginning.

Rollo himself came from Norway although he had been outlawed from that country and had settled for a time in Ireland. The Vikings he now led were nearly all Danish. The land he had given to him was pleasant and fertile, with a long coastline so that his Vikings were never far from the sea. It had been Christian for six centuries but never had a name, for it had merely been part of the Frankish kingdom. In time the settlement became known as 'the land of the Northmen' and sometime in the early part of the 11th century it became simply—Normandy.

By then Rollo, the original Viking leader, had founded a line of Dukes of Normandy with high-sounding names.

A Viking "pays homage" to Charles the Simple

They were William I Longsword, Richard the Fearless, Richard II the Good, his son Richard III who ruled for such a short time he did not have time to acquire a further name, and Robert the Magnificent.

This last duke was the father of a son called William. The child was born to a girl called Arlette, daughter of a tanner of Falaise. When he was older, William was accepted by the nobles as Robert's heir, after his father, the duke, had died whilst returning from Jerusalem in 1035.

William became Duke of Normandy in the same year and, thirty-one years later, this descendant of a Norse Viking gained an even greater title. By right of arms he became William I of England . . . William the Conqueror.

THE VIKING HERITAGE

REFERRING TO the Viking raids on his country, an old Irish monk wrote:

"Although there were an hundred heads of hardened iron on one neck, and an hundred sharp, ready, cool, never rusting, brazen tongues in each head, and an hundred garrulous loud, unceasing voices from each tongue, they could not recount or narrate or enumerate or tell what all the Haedeal (Irish) suffered in common, both men and women, laity and clergy, old and young, noble and ignoble, of hardship and of injuring and oppressing in every house, from those valiant, wrathful, purely pagan people".

The Isle of Man suffered frequently at the hands of Vikings. The owner of this sword, a 9th century Scandinavian chieftain, was buried there

This was typical of the "bad press" the Vikings had, for the chroniclers of the time were mainly churchmen who hated the 'pagans' and delighted in writing of their cruelty and ruthlessness. There was, however, much truth in what they wrote, for between the 9th and 11th centuries the Vikings were the "bogey-men" of Europe.

But there was far more to the Vikings than their desire for adventure, excitement and gold. Today, because of the important archaeological finds and the translation of their heroic poetry and the Icelandic prose sagas, they stand revealed in a completely new light. They were undoubtedly the greatest explorers and settlers of the age. From Norway they sailed north of the Scottish Mainland to settle in north-west England, Scotland, Ireland, the Shetlands, Orkneys, Faroes and the Isle of Man, Iceland and Greenland. They were also the first Europeans to set foot in America. The Danes took their long-

Part of a woven wall hanging depicting the conversion of Swedish Vikings to Christianity and the end of the Viking Age

ships into the North Sea and the English Channel to settle in the east and north-east of England, and in Normandy; the Swedes took the river route from the Baltic to the Caspian and Black Seas.

Owing to their hardy upbringing and self-discipline they were mostly tall and strong, with well muscled bodies and features as handsome as those of the ancient Greeks. They believed in courage, loyalty and justice, they had a great appreciation of beautiful things, and their craftsmanship was unique.

Although it is a thousand years and more since the Vikings began to settle, the names they gave to their homes and

UNIVERSITETETS OLDSAKSAMLING, OSLO

Symbol of the Vikings' rare craftsmanship in wood: a staring, bearded warrior, from the cart found at the Oseberg ship burial

settlements still exist. Throughout England such endings as "by" and "thorpe" are an indication of such places: for example, Wetherby (Yorks) meaning "Wether village"; Whitby (Yorks)—"White village"; Bagthorpe (Norfolk)—"Bakki's homestead" and many, many more.

The Vikings left behind numerous traces of a vigorous civilisation which reveals their intelligence, energy and adaptability. Despite what the old monks may have written, they had a great personal code of honour and were concerned about the opinions of others. In the words of Hávamál:

> *Cattle die, kinsfolk die,*
> *We ourselves must die.*
> *One thing will never die—*
> *The dead man's reputation.*

STATENS HISTORISKA MUSEUM, STOCKHOLM

A picture stone serving as memorial to an unknown Viking ship. Clearly identifiable are the sailors' chain mail tunics and the network of ropes reinforcing the sail

91

Index

Figures in italics refer to illustrations

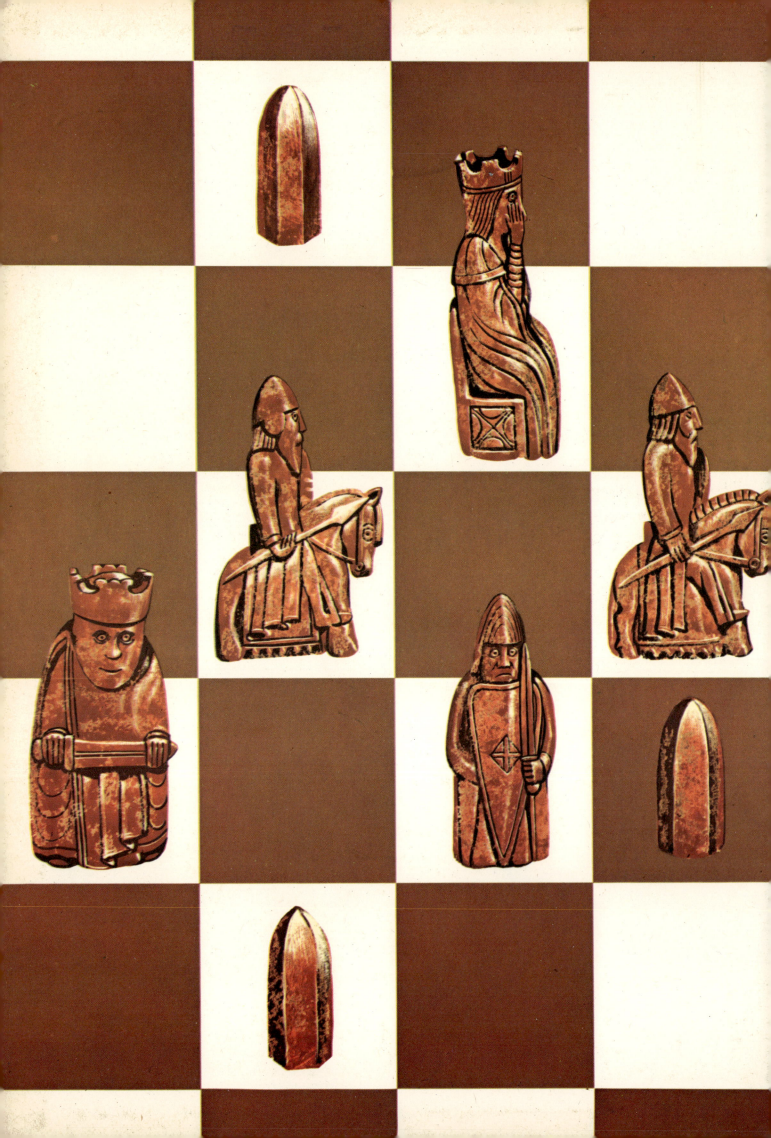